Burns '84 USA

Presented to

R BRUCE WHIELLANS

By

NATIONAL TRUST
FOR SCOTLAND

LANARKSHIRE
MEMBERS GROUP

PICKERING & INGLIS LTD.   PRINTED IN GREAT BRITAIN

Stanley Baxter's bedside book of Glasgow humour

STANLEY BAXTER'S
bedside book of
Glasgow humour

Stanley Baxter

with Alex Mitchell

Constable·London

First published in Great Britain 1986
by Constable and Company Limited
10 Orange Street London WC2H 7EG
Copyright © 1986 Stanley Baxter and Alex Mitchell
Set in Linotron Sabon 12pt by
Rowland Phototypesetting Ltd
Bury St Edmunds, Suffolk
Printed in Great Britain by
St Edmundsbury Press Ltd
Bury St Edmunds, Suffolk

British Library CIP data
Baxter, Stanley
Stanley Baxter's bedside book of Glasgow
humour
I. Title   II. Mitchell, Alex, 1906–
828'.91407   PR6052.A84/

ISBN 0 09 467270 9

Contents

Foreword

When Alex Mitchell and I were writing the first *Parliamo Glasgow* script for TV transmission (in Scotland only) we had some misgivings about its acceptability in other parts of Scotland. 'Is it *too* Glaswegian?' we asked ourselves. The enormous success of that first sketch all over Scotland made me realise that Glaswegian is the *lingua franca* of Scottish comedy. Everybody in Scotland seems to love it, and it is perhaps for this reason that the biggest names in Scottish comedy have almost all been from the Glasgow area.

I think the rest of Scotland has a wistful envy of the Glaswegian's extrovert outlook on life. I have never found fellow Scots from whatever part of Scotland 'dour' or 'mean', two of the very unfair adjectives commonly applied to us. But there tends to be a quiet reserve and caution allied with patient mental application that has won the trust of southerners for Scots as doctors and financial advisers.

But the typical Glaswegian has scant regard for caution or reserve. He is totally at the other end of the emotional spectrum. Extrovert, talkative, argumentative and often over-generous with money, the Glaswegian is the opposite of the world's Scots stereotype.

Is it because of the tremendous numbers of Glaswegians of Irish descent? Possibly. Something of the same temperament can be discerned in Liverpool, which has a similar social history, and there are marked similarities in the humour of both cities. Both are iconoclastic and cynical and both with a voracious appetite for the absurd. The more surrealistically absurd the better.

I'm just old enough to have seen the legendary Scots comedian Tommy Lorne, and have all his gramophone records, save one, on tape. Lorne didn't represent (like Tommy Morgan) the extrovert 'gallus' Glaswegian. He was his victim.

In a wonderful sketch he played an apprentice undertaker being instructed on how to solicit business in the American manner. A dynamic briefing from his 'straight man' on door-to-door salesmanship for undertaking takes place. It must be reverend, subtle and not give offence. Just some solicitous enquiries as to the general health of each household visited.

Lorne and his boss are standing in front of three doors in a stage 'cloth'. They are dressed in full undertaker rig – including black crêpe round their funeral top hats. So we know the enterprise is doomed.

The guffaws begin as anticipation mounts. Lorne approaches the first door and knocks. It is answered by a big Glasgow 'bruiser'. In his famous apologetic whine Lorne enquires, 'Have you any bodies?'.

He is set upon by the irate householder and his top hat jumped upon as a *coup de grâce*. After each disastrous call he is reprimanded, rebriefed and has another go. Physical assault is his lot on every occasion. No wonder Glaswegians loved it! Physical violence, a big 'jessie' of a man trying to cope with it, and the subject – death.

Of course death is no longer a taboo subject in the South but all Scots had a great fondness for it when it was still considered in the rest of Britain as not a subject for laughs. Although sex jokes were always received with considerable unease by Scots we were very brave about facing up to the other realities of life. We have a stronger stomach for it.

In the days when I was still working in repertory at the Citizens Theatre our annual pantomime was largely left in my hands for its comic content. In one item Molly Urquhart and I played two Glasgow waitresses who were both unhygienic and illiterate. Molly realised that her partner would have the edge on her for laughs because, after all, I was in drag and she wasn't. Women especially tend to find drag funnier.

Molly solved the problem by creating a gothic horror of a woman that nobody could obliterate from the memory. She not only brought her shoulders up to her ears in a frightening hump, but acquired a cleft palate. To round off the portrayal she crossed her eyes and *kept* them crossed for the nine-minute duration of the sketch.

After the dress rehearsal our recently-appointed and somewhat effete English producer came backstage and said, 'Oh, you can't seriously expect anyone to laugh at that disgusting sketch about the waitresses. It's too, too horrible. Can we take it out please?'. I think its removal

over my deceased body was mentioned and he reluctantly agreed to try it on an audience. The hysteria with which it was greeted left our 'artistic director' stunned. 'Oh, I'll never understand Glasgow audiences', he groaned.

The truth is that comedy is not about pleasant things. It's about frightening and tragic and sordid things exorcised by looking at them comedically. The really big laughs come when the comedian successfully walks a tightrope over an abyss of bad taste. Glaswegians – perhaps more than most – hope he'll fall.

Stanley Baxter

Introduction

Rough irony, scathing scepticism and a dogged defiance of the rules of English grammar and diction. These are the main ingredients of Glasgow humour.

The division between the classes is deep. Residents of what estate agents call 'exclusive' suburbs do not mix socially with what used to be called the working-class citizens.

A certain animosity manifests itself when these different types of Glaswegian chance to meet. This is illustrated by the tale, possibly apocryphal, of two ladies from Glasgow's oldest and richest suburb, Pollokshields, who, during a shopping expedition, dropped in to an unpretentious cafe for afternoon tea.

On the table in front of them were the remains of

someone's meal. It was a round pie from which the filling had been removed.

'Look at thet, Engela,' said the genteel matron, 'Someone must hev lost their eppetite.' A waitress hoovering nearby heard the remark and explained, 'It wizny that, missus. It wiz an auld fella that ordered the pie. But he only ett the middle o' it. He couldny get his gums through the crusty bit.'

'He was eating with his *gums*?' exclaimed one of the ladies in astonishment.

'That's right,' agreed the waitress, 'He'd came oot wi'oot his wallies.'

The matrons were surprised that anyone would venture forth without their wallies, or dentures. Not a few Glaswegians dispense with their painful lower denture.

Artificial teeth are a frequent subject of sardonic jest in Glasgow. A gent with dentures that are too unrealistically white may be accused of having 'The Great Wall o' China in his mooth'.

Strong drink comes in for considerable comment from Glaswegians. A citizen who is intoxicated may be said to be 'bevvied', 'miroclous', 'jaked', 'stovin'' 'bung fu'' or 'as fu' as a whulk'.

Females who drink to excess meet with strong disapproval. There is the sad story of the young lady who drank too many toasts at a wedding reception. 'Her fiance Big Boab was seein' her hame when she fell. He accidentally tramped on her hand an' broke all the gless in her engagemint ring.'

Death is joked about by all Scots, especially by Glaswegians. So we have the sorry tale told by a damsel about her aunt who appears to have been accident-prone.

'Ma Aunty Jenny was comin' hame fae the bingo when somethin' came over her,' recounted the young lady. 'It was a double-decker bus. She lost baith her legs. But she was fittit wi' a perra widdin' wans by the National Health. She managed fine wi' them until wan night her chip-pan caught fire and set the hoose ablaze. The hoose wasn't badly damaged but ma aunty was burnt tae the ground.'

Another lady, a rather faded spinster, and a friend attended the funeral of a friend's husband. 'That's the fourth husband Bella's had cremated,' remarked the friend.

'Wid ye credit that!' exclaimed the spinster, 'Ah canny get a man an' she's burnin' them!'

Sectarianism is also the cause of ribaldry in the city. The neighbours disapproved of Big Hughie's choice of bride. 'It's wan o' thae mixed marriages,' the lady disclosed. 'He's fae Glasgow an' she's fae Edinburgh.'

It was at a wedding that I first became aware of the Glaswegian habit of substituting 'r' for the 'th' sound. The bride's brother was called upon for a song. With great feeling he rendered an old ballad which went 'I can hear ra mavis singin' his love-song to ra wurld.'

The sentimental ditty 'The Star o' Rabbie Burns' is often rendered 'Rastara Rabbieburns'.

Violent, as well as natural death, is the subject of Glasgow humour. It is related that a large poster headed 'Man Wanted For Murder' was posted outside a city police station ... and 200 men applied for the job.

The predicament of a short-tempered housewife who struck and killed her husband with a frying-pan is reported. She rushed from her 10th-storey abode and shouted to a neighbour 'Oh, Aggie, Ah've jist killed ma man! Ah'll be charged wi' murder an' get life!' Aggie, a lady of resource, urged her to keep calm. 'Jist go back tae the hoose,' she advised. 'Pit a wet chamois cloth in his haun' an' fling him oot the windae.'

To make things easier for non-Glaswegian readers I have indulged heavily in phoneticization as in the following tale which demonstrates what a conversation sounds like when 'r' is substituted for the 't' and 'th'.

The story concerns a young woman and her parents who were walking home after visiting the home of friends in the early hours of the New Year. The trio had not gone far before the father sat down suddenly on the pavement. His daughter inquired of her mother, 'Heh, murra, whit's the marra wi' ma farra?' Her mother informed her that her father cannot go any farther — 'Yur farra canny go nae furra.' She points to a barrow and suggests that they put the overtired gent on it and wheel him home. 'Erra barra owrerr. We'll pirrim oan it an' hurlim hame.'

That is just one example of the picturesque language in which the humour of the native Glaswegian is conveyed.

1 *The Windae-Hingers*

Some Glasgow housewives possess an acute sense of observation and a liking for commenting, sometimes acidly, on people and events.

Two female neighbours, as often as not known by the familiar Glasgow names 'Serah' and 'Maggie', appear simultaneously at adjacent tenement windows which are wide open. Each is seated and her elbows are placed on a cushion on the window sill.

They exchange the traditional Glasgow greetings. Says Serah – 'Yur therr' ('you are there'), to which Maggie responds with, 'Oh shursel' ('Oh it is yourself').

Then they indulge in what is known as a 'hing' – i.e. a hang out of the window – and their commentary is usually made in tones of disapproval, something like the following:

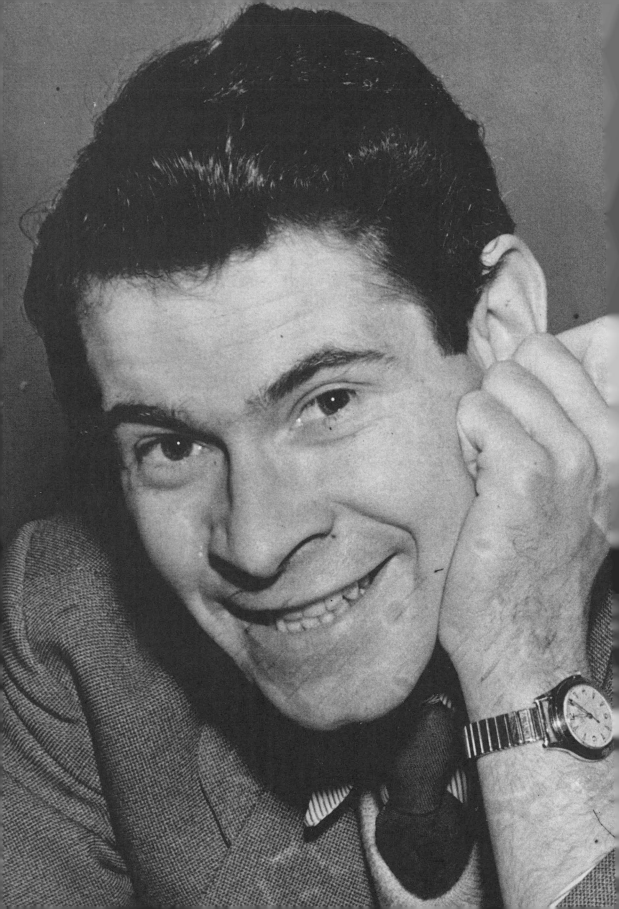

SERAH:	Did ye get home a'right fae the licensed grocers' dance?
MAGGIE:	Aye, but Wullie strained his back helpin' me alang the street.
SERAH:	Puir wee sowl. Ye shoulda took a taxi.
MAGGIE:	Ach Ah wiz walkin' fine till Wullie lost his grip oan me.
SERAH:	It's ages since there wiz ony excitement in the street.
MAGGIE:	No' since yon night when Big Bella McLeish was threw oot the pub at the corner an' landit oan Wee Mrs McGravie.
SERAH:	That Bella McLeish gives hur man the life o' a dug. She gives him Pal Meat an' egg fur his brekfast an' Pal Meat sangwidges fur his dinner an' tea.
MAGGIE:	Aye, they say he ett that much Pal Meat he couldny pass a lamp-post.
SERAH:	Oh therr's Michelle McGuffie. A nice wee lassie but she dizny look too weel.
MAGGIE:	Naw she dizny. Hur murra got the doctor tae her. He tell't hur 'Ye canny expec' tae feel weel if ye work all day an' dance in the disco all night.' There was nothin' fur it, she hud tae gi'e up hur joab.
SERAH:	Ah'm told she wiz engaged tae a young French fella she met in Majorca. He hud luvly manners. But every time he kissed hur hand he burnt his nose on her fag. Then wan day he went tae kiss her an' her bubblegum burst in his face. He began tae look down his nose at hur. So she broke it aff.

MAGGIE: Karen Bolgeton's became engaged.
SERAH: Oh who huz SHE nabbed?
MAGGIE: Hur financy's very well-off. But he's nearly seventy years auld.
SERAH: D'ye mean she's gonny marry a man that's three times aulder than hur?
MAGGIE: That's right. An' ye know whit'll happen when she marries him.
SERAH: Naw, whit?
MAGGIE: She'll find auld age creepin' over her.
SERAH: Therr's that toaffy-nosed big wumman fae the top flat. She'll be goin' tae meet hur posh freens.
MAGGIE: Whit's that she's got oan hur hauns? Ma Goad, it's GLOVES!
SERAH: So it is! She'll be werrin' a hat nixt instead o' that bedmat she calls a heidscarf. Is that Maisie McTurk's lassie on the urra side o' the street?
MAGGIE: Aye, that's Karen. A right nice lassie. Very mannerly, an' very clever tae.
SERAH: So she is. She's no' like the other young yins. SHE's no' enjoyin' the teachers' strike. She's dain' hur lessons at hame!
MAGGIE: Aye, hur murra wiz tellin' me that. She says Karen's learnt hersel' English grammar.
SERAH: She'll grow up tae be a lady.
MAGGIE: So she will. She's very ladylike a'readies.
SERAH: She's saw us. She's lookin' up at us.
(Karen shouts up at the two ladies)
KAREN: Away an' get waashed, ya perra bliddy goassips!
MAGGIE: Oh here, she's no' as ladylike as Ah thought!

2 Bachles, Nyaffs, Dreeps, etc

Glaswegians are intensely interested in the physical aspects of their fellow citizens. Any male approaching six feet in height has 'big' before his name as in Big Hughie and Big Wullie. A female of five feet is 'wee' as in Wee Samantha and Wee Polly.

These descriptions are bestowed with a certain affection. The Glaswegian reserves more picturesque words for those who meet with his or her disapproval. A small unkempt individual is known as a bachle. The bachles are invariably diminutive with clothes that are a size or two too large for them. Females are never described as bachles. A small ill-dressed girl or woman bears the derogatory cognomen of 'gether-up' or is known as a 'huddery tramp'.

The 'ch' in bachle is pronounced as in the Scottish word 'loch'. Scots shudder when they hear an English person speaking of 'Lock Lomond'.

The word 'bachle' should not be confused with 'bauchle'. A bauchle is a worn-out shoe. A bachle wearing bauchles may result in his having a stumbling gait and would be described as a 'shachly bachle'.

Such a person is, naturally enough, not looked upon with favour by the fair sex. A bachle who tries to make the acquaintance of a damsel may be requested to put himself forward as a prize in a lottery. 'Awa' an' raffle yursel' ya wee bachle,' she will say.

Bachles are always undersized. One never hears of a big bachle. A tall, shabbily-dressed gent is known contemptuously as a 'big dreep'.

Big Pam's marriage to Wee Danny came in for adverse comment from the notorious gossips, Maggie and Serah:

'Ah don't know whit she seen in the wee bachle,' said Maggie. 'He's no' the size o' tuppence.'

'Ah bet he wiz all she could get,' Serah informed her. 'She wiz that long on the shelf she hud coarns oan hur bahookie.'

'Hur man's a right handy size,' Maggie went on, 'When she gets annoyed wi' him she jist shoves him in the loabby press.'

A nyaff is also a diminutive male. But he differs in temperament from the bachle. Whereas the bachle is self-effacing, the nyaff is self-assured, even aggressive. It is said of him that he 'fancies his barra'.

One forward five-footer in a discotheque was disappointed in his partner's lack of Terpsichorean prowess. 'Ye can dance hee-haw,' he told her. His comment was met with the scathing response, 'Awa' an' jine Snowhite an' the urra six dwarfs, ya cheeky little nyuck.'

Another diminutive gent who attempted to push past a large matron in a bus queue was threatened by her with a painful operation. 'Ya impiddint wee nyaff! Staun' back or Ah'll skite the face aff ye!'

Males who become too ebullient after partaking of too many refreshments also come in for condemnation. They are known as 'heidcases' or 'heidbangers'.

Extreme contempt and ribaldry is reserved for any of the above-mentioned category of citizen who is brave enough to wear a hairpiece.

So the story is told of Wee Baldy Bain, a bald bachle who lost his hairpiece. 'His wig blew aff in Sauchiehall Street,' reported an eye-witness. 'He ran efter it an' he wiz haufway atae Edinburgh afore he fun' he wiz chasin' a Pekinese dug.'

Certain physical characteristics have their own picturesque nomenclature. A person with a particularly round cranium will find it likened to a ball or turnip and is known as 'bawheid' or 'tumshie-skull'. Had Cromwell and his followers operated in Scotland they, no doubt, would have been dubbed 'Cromwell and his Bawheids'.

A Glaswegian gallant was annoyed to hear this romantic description of his sweetheart. A false friend maintained, 'He calls her his "melancholy baby", that's because she's goat a heid like a melon an' a face like a collie.'

Unkind remarks are also suffered by maidens whose legs are not as straight as they might be. She is described, not as bow-legged, but 'bowlly' as in the sentence, 'She's that bowlly she can walk on baith sides of the street at the same time.'

Even feet, or 'spuds' as they are called, are jeered at if

they are unduly large. So we have the unkind statement, 'Her spuds are that big she goat a job with the Ministry of Agriculture stampin' oot forest fires.'

Those are just a few of the strange words and phrases that enrich the patois of the great city on the Clyde. Others, even more bizarre, will come from the characters featuring in the chapters that follow.

3   *Ladies from outer space*

Somebody once asked me – a Sassenach of course – 'What's the difference between Kelvinside and Morningside?', as if referring to two districts in the same city. Morningside is the Edinburgh 'twin' of Kelvinside as far as comedians are concerned.

In jokes the districts are interchangeable for they both have the same reputation for striving to be well-spoken and ultra genteel. But visually there is no comparison. Morningside matrons represent 'old money'. It might have been great-grandfather who owned the brewery or printing works and there may not be very much left in the bank in cash and shares – nevertheless appearances must be maintained, and no matter that a fur coat is thirty years old: it was a good one, and will do nicely.

Both the ladies and their menfolk are devoted to Scottish tweeds — always aristocratically baggy and worn. All over Edinburgh retired bank managers and advocates are to be seen in a motley assortment of country headgear in which a Glasgow business man wouldn't be seen dead. They may be standing at a bus stop in Princes Street but the inference is that they are in town for the day and the estate is somewhere in the borders or in Fife.

Not at all. They are returning to their terraced Morningside house with a fourth estimate for roof repairs in the pocket of their Inverness cape.

Glasgow — with its obsession with modernity, its longing to be 'hip' — finds all this dowdy. I've grown to love Edinburgh but as a child I was warned before a day trip to the capital that it simply couldn't be compared with Glasgow. My mother would wave an airy hand as we walked along Princes Street and say 'This is all it's got — there's not much else', thus dismissing the New Town, the Adams Brothers and the whole mediaeval legacy on the Castle side of that famous street.

Life to a Glaswegian is Argylle Street on a Saturday afternoon: the Byres Road bustle, the Charing Cross chaos. And Kelvinside matrons — the term would be anathema to them — are into the latest hairdos and outfits that *avoid* tweed and flirt with *Dynasty*. They are, in short, more raffish altogether.

We lived in North Kelvinside — a district nearer Maryhill Road than Kelvinside proper — and lived in a tenement 3-up on your right. But it was a big flat with its cornices and ceiling roses and there we enjoyed a live-in maid who would serve afternoon tea to my mother's lady friends as they played ma-jongh in the parlour. All spoke in the classic Kelvinside accent, with its uvular 'r'.

*　　*　　*

28

My writing partner Alex and I had female relatives who spoke with authentic Glasgow suburban accents. We continued our studies by frequent visits to a tea-room in Daly's, a fashionable Sauchiehall Street dress shop, a favourite haunt of the genteel ladies. The tables were quite close to one another, enabling us to eavesdrop. On several occasions we witnessed the battle of the bills. The battlers bore such names as Jainnifer and Sendra. Who was to pay for the afternoon tea was hotly contested in the following manner:

SANDRA:	Jainnifer, it's MAI turn to get the bill. You paid lest taime.
JENNIFER:	No, YOU paid. It's MAI turn today. Anyway you paid for the sherries at lunch.
SANDRA:	But thet was just mai treat to you for lending me your stole for Deirdre McCallum's waidding.
JENNIFER:	Ai insist on paying for the tea.
SANDRA:	Jainnifer McMurtrie, give me thet bill or ai'll never come out with you again.
JENNIFER:	Oh well, here you are, take it. You're an awful girl, Sendra! What's thet? You've nothing less than a twainty-pound note? Och, Ai've change, AI'LL pay.

An airy manner and a certain lack of tact are characteristic of some genteel Glasgow suburban ladies.

Such a one is Maureen. The following account of her niece, Caroline's wedding is typical of her genre:

'Caroline's waidding went off quite well. Maind you, Ai thought that her waidding-gown looked a wee

bitty tight on her. Oh mai, you don't think she's . . .
och no, she's only known Derek for two months.

He's really quite a naice boy. It just shows you – you
can't judge from appearances. His father's quite well
off. He was telling Elistair that he does extensive trade
with China. We found out later that he manufactures
potties.

Ai asked Caroline where she was going on her
honeymoon. "Oh," she said, "Derek was thinking of
Interlaken."

Ai told her MAI bridegroom could think of nothing
else.

The reception was ebsolutely marvellous, only the
bridegroom's mother got a wee bit fu'! Ai don't think
she's used to champagne. She insisted on doing a
Spanish dance. It was a wee bit of a shock when one of
her heels came off and she skited along the floor and
landed on top of wee Mrs Mathieson.

My hubby Elistair enjoyed himself too. Maind you,
Ai don't think rum and champagne mix awfully well.
But Ai'll say this for Elistair, he always knows when
he's had enough; he just falls flet on his beck.

Ai believe the young couple eventually decaided to
go on honeymoon to Spain – to Forrosima, the charm-
ing wee village Elistair end Ai were at lest year.

Ai hope Caroline end Derek enjoy it there. We got
quite used to the drains and the plagues of flies and
mosquitoes but we weren't awfully keen on the lizards
and scorpions. Still, Ai suppose you've got to put up
with these things when you go abroad.

Well, Ai'd better toddle off now. Ai've got to collect
Elistair's prescription at the chemist's. It's for tablets
for his haigh blood pressure. Ai cain't for the life of me
understand what raises his blood pressure. Bai-bai.'

4 *They only serve*

In my tea and coffee-swilling days in Glasgow I was fascinated by the waitresses in some of the city's smaller establishments. These young ladies are a race apart. Their delightful informality often astonishes customers from south of the Border.

Unlike their counterparts in London, the Glasgow waitress rarely, if ever, addresses a male customer as 'sir'. Nor does she favour a female with the title 'madam'.

Nevertheless the Glasgow waitress is most attentive and friendly. But heaven help the customer who attempts to high-hat her.

The story, possibly apocryphal, is told of two snobbish suburban ladies in a down-market café who summoned the waitress to their table with imperious and impatient calls of 'Miss!'.

The girl ambled over to them and was told by one of the ladies, 'Bring us a pot of tea for two and make sure that I get a clean cup.'

The waitress gave her a glare of hatred and sauntered off. Some twenty minutes later she was back with a tray on which were a tiny teapot and two cups and saucers.

'Here ye are,' she rasped. 'Which wan o' yiz waantit the clean cup?'

Two of my favourite waitresses in Glasgow were Gloria and Clara. They were wont to get together quite close to where I sat and exchange views on the various patrons of the tea-room. The following sketch gives some idea of their conversation:

GLORIA: Whit the hell are YOU daen' in sae early?
CLARA: Ah've been huntin' aboot in the kitchen.
GLORIA: Whit huv ye been huntin' fur?
CLARA: That big lumpa toffy the chef gave me yesterday. Ah've loast it.
GLORIA: Ach the chef'll gi'e ye anurra wan.
CLARA: Naw, Ah waant the lumpa toffy Ah hud yesterday.
GLORIA: Why?
CLARA: Ma tap denchur's in it . . . Ach Ah'm fed up wi' this place.
GLORIA: Me tae. Ah wiz faur happier in the chip shope servin' lang tatties an' big peas.
CLARA: Here, Gloria.
GLORIA: Whit is it, Clerra?
CLARA: Why dae they ca' this place 'The Jungle Room'?
GLORIA: It's obvious, the manager's a beast. D'ye know whit he hud the cheek tae say tae me yesterday?

CLARA:	No. Whit?
GLORIA:	He sayed he wanted me tae show a bit more decorum . . . I said I was showin' enough already.
CLARA:	Ye know, Gloria, there's times Ah don't like men. The chef's no' speakin' tae me, ye know.
GLORIA:	Why not?
CLARA:	He heard a customer askin' me fur the chef's special. I sayed – 'The big blonde waitress doesnae come in till six a' cloke.'
GLORIA:	We'll be late again the night wi' that big reunion party.
CLARA:	The one they're gettin' in a' the pies an' cans o' beer fur?
GLORIA:	Aye.
CLARA:	Whose reunion party is it?
GLORIA:	The former pupils o' thon posh school in the West End. . . . Aw, here's a coupla mugs! (*Man and girl enter and sit down at Gloria's table. Clara and Gloria stand together with folded arms, looking balefully at the couple.*)
GLORIA:	Damn nuisance comin' in as early as this!
CLARA:	Ah wouldnae like tae be kissed with a moustache like THAT!
GLORIA:	Ah'll bet ye he's goat sparras nestin' in it!
MAN:	I say . . . Miss! (*Gloria glowers at him.*)
GLORIA:	Did you say somethin'?
MAN:	Well actually we've come in for . . .
GLORIA:	Were ye wantin' somethin'?
MAN:	I want the menu card.
CLARA:	(*Calls over to him*) It's in front o' ye.

MAN: (*Picking up card*) Really! (*He scans card.
            As Gloria waits she pulls up her skirt and
            scratches the back of her thigh. Man looks
            down, surprised.*)

GLORIA: Never mind THAT! Whit d'ye want tae
            EAT?

MAN: What? Oh. (*Looks at menu card again*)
            Where is the ravioli?

GLORIA: The WHIT?

MAN: The ravioli. Where is the ravioli?

GLORIA: Oh it's the second on the left past the
            pillar.

MAN: What nonsense! Bring us some soup, ANY
            kind of soup.

GLORIA: Are ye SURE ye want soup?

MAN: Of course we're sure! (*To his companion*)
            YOU want soup, don't you darling?
            (*She simpers and nods.*)

GLORIA: (*Going to Clara*) He wants soup! And
            darling wants soup. Heh Susie! Two plates
            o' yer sheepdip!
            (*The plates are handed to Gloria and she
            takes them to man and girl and sets them
            down.*)

MAN: Good heavens, you had your thumb in my
            soup!

GLORIA: Och it's all right. The soup's no' hot.

GIRL: I think I'm going to have the condiments.

GLORIA: (*To Clara*) Oh my, she's gonny be seeck!

MAN: The lady wants the pepper and salt! Where
            are they?
            (*Tugs at his moustache*).

GLORIA: Aw keep yer soup-strainer on! Clerra,
            bring the pepper an' sau't.

	(*Clara picks up pepper and salt pots from her table and sprinkles the plates of soup heavily. Man and girl sneeze.*)
MAN:	Dammit, we could do that ourselves!
CLARA:	No ye cannae. We've only got the wan cruet here.
GLORIA:	Ye're no' in the Holiday Inn noo. (*Man and girl taste soup and grimace.*)
MAN:	My God! Take this muck away. I want something to eat. Bring me the manager!
CLARA:	Would ye credit that! He's a cannybile! (*Takes away the soup plates.*)
GLORIA:	Ye cannae see the manager. He's went oot for his lunch. What d'ye want tae follow — apart fae Lady Godiva therr?
MAN:	This is ridiculous! (*Gives menu card to girl.*) Darling, YOU choose something. (*She points at something on the card.*) All right. (*To Gloria*) We'll have curry and rice and potato croquettes.
GLORIA:	Curry and rice and potato croquettes?
MAN:	Yes.
GLORIA:	(*With dark foreboding*) Okay, you asked for it. Right, Susie! Two bus drivers' specials an' tattie crockets! (*Two plates are handed out to her.*) Whit's THIS, Susie? Oh, the curry an' rice? (*Laughs*) Ah thought it was two durty dish-towels! (*Takes plates of curry and rice to man and girl. Then she calls to Clara*) Bring the tattie crockets, Clerra.
CLARA:	Ah'm comin', Gloria. (*A shet of croquettes with serving tongs are handed to her from the side.*) Oh ma Goad, this is hoat! (*She*

GLORIA: *(rushes to couple's table and bangs down the ashet on it.)* Oh ma fingers is burnin'! *(Blows on fingers and wrings hands.)*

GLORIA: *(Touching ashet)* Oh, it's rid hoat! Wherr's the tongs? *(Takes up tongs)* Ur YOU fur a crocket, miss? *(Girl nods and Gloria picks up a croquette with the tongs. It falls from them.)* Oh here, wherr did that yin go? *(The girl rises and reveals it has fallen down her decolletage; she rises, wriggles and wails with agony.)*

MAN: *(Rising) (To Gloria)* You utter fool! *(He is about to put his hand down the front of the girl's dress to retrieve it. Gloria smacks his hand away.)*

GLORIA: Stop that, ya durty auld rascal. I'll get it! *(Clara runs off and returns with a siphon of soda water. Gloria tries to reach the croquette with the tongs.)* You want tae watch this fella. Ye don't waant tae end up in the *News of the World* . . . Haud still. *(Gloria is still struggling to retrieve the croquette when Clara returns with the soda siphon. She directs a jet down the front of the girl's dress.)*

CLARA: Therr ye are, dear. Ye're all right now.

GLORIA: *(To girl.)* It wiz jist a wee accident. We'll no' charge ye fur the crocket.

CLARA: An' the sody watter's free tae.

MAN: This is outrageous! We've had nothing to eat!

GLORIA: It's too late noo, Bawheid.

MAN: What do you mean – too late?

GLORIA: It's oor hauf–day. Come oan, Clerra!

5 Off the chain

Sixty years ago a local historian wrote – 'Glasgow Fair has been unfailingly observed under circumstances that have greatly changed with the times.' Well, in those days you could travel from Glasgow to Rothesay and back for five shillings, the old-fashioned term for 25p.

Doon the Watter! What magic memories that pretty phrase conjures up. The city's railway stations on Fair Saturday morning, the air ringing with such spirited holiday cries as –

'Huv ye no' brung the sangwidges?'
'Keepa haudera wean!'
'Lift that case aff ma fit!'
'He's furgoat the tickets!'

'Ah'll nougitt wafer ye!'
'Ye've nae time tae go a place!'
'Ma Goad, we're in the wrang train!'

and, of course,

'It's rainin' like hell noo!'

And at the Broomielaw, where hundreds embarked on the steamers for the sail downriver to the Clyde resorts, similar observations could be heard –

'He went doon tae see the ingines an' goat weel-oiled.'
'It's too blowy up at the sherp end o' the boaat.'
'Ach look whit that seagull's did tae ma new blazer!'

Then the arrival at that paradise known to generations of Glasgow vacationists as 'Roassy'.
How exciting it was – fully-fashioned ladies being stuck on the gangway, small men struggling with large suitcases, laughin' lassies and wailin' weans ... all engulfed in that entrancing aroma that permeated the pier, a mélange of fish and chips, ozone and petrol fumes.
Later came the stroll along the promenade with the traditional Glasgow Fair salutations –

'Fancy meetin' YOU!'
'Hullo ... Ah see yer bunions is still botherin' ye.'
'Luvly day, intit? ... Ah'm hurryin' away tae the bingo.'
'Ye can walk here fur miles an' no' see a pub.'

Alas, the holiday hordes from Glasgow no longer descend on Rothesay in July. The certainty of constant sunshine has made them switch their allegiance to Spain.

Magaluf or Majorca has become 'Glesca on the Med'. But all does not go smoothly with Glaswegians in foreign parts. So one hears such complaints as –

'Ah'm seeck o' this dampt scaampi. Whit wid Ah no' give fur a big poke o' fish an' chips.'
'Maggie's feart tae go oot. Hur face is as rid as a furnace efter lyin' in the sun.'

And the course of romance does not always run smoothly for the Glaswegian damsels:

'He's a smashin' lookin' guy right anough. But he's that ignurint. He can only speak Spanish. Ah huvny managed tae learn him ony English yit.'

My suburban friend Jennifer and her husband Alistair favoured the most exclusive Spanish resort, Marbella. Here we see her showing, to her friend Maureen, snap-shots she took there:

'The snaps have come out awfly well, Mawreen. Here's one of Elistair on the beach. He didn't lie there long. He'd caught a tummy bug the day before and a doctor in the hotel gave him some tablets and told him – "These'll keep you going". You can guess where they kept him going *to*.
'Oh, this is a couple we met at the marina. They had a lovely house there and their own yacht. They were really quite well-to-do and we became quite friendly with them until a man we got talking to in the hotel bar

told us about the man. It seems he had embezzled £40,000 in England.

'Oh, this is one Ai took of Deirdre, you know, the girl who lives at the end of our avenue. Ai was a bit taken aback when Ai saw SHE was in Marbella. Ai've always thought she had a wee notion of Elistair and Ai think he rather liked her. So Ai took these snaps of Deirdre on the beach and showed them to Elistair. She's got a nerve wearing a bikini. Look at her lying there like a stranded whale. It's amazing how those skinny legs can support that huge body. This one shows her bending down to pick up her bathrobe. Did you ever see such a big bottie? Here's one of the hotels. It'll look quite nice when the scaffolding's removed. You know, a workman climbed up that scaffolding three storeys and looked in at my bathroom window while Ai was in the bath . . . Mind you, he was very polite. He stood there apologising for twenty minutes.'

The traditional Glaswegian holiday cries differ from country to country. In Spain the warm sunshine is acclaimed with such heartfelt exclamations as 'SELLU-VAHOAT' or 'AMFERRBILIN'.

In Scottish resorts the holiday weather is greeted with such Gaelic-sounding calls as 'SCUMMINDOONIN! SCUMMINDOONIN BUCKITS!' or simply, 'AMBLID-DIDROOKIT!'

Glaswegians enter with enthusiasm into the holiday spirit and they give pious thanks for life with cries of 'Allah! Allah! . . . 'ALLAHWAFURRAHAUF!' or 'ALLAHWAFURRAPINT!'

6 *The dancers*

About a half-century ago Glasgow prided itself on being 'The dancingest city in Europe'. Its inhabitants, young and old, flocked to the city's thirty-odd dance halls.

Admission prices ranged from 1/6d (7½ pence) to 7/6d (37½ pence). It was in the less expensive halls that true Glaswegian fun was to be had.

In these more down-market haunts the young female patrons congregated at one end of the hall and the males, known as 'solo men', gathered at the other end keenly surveying prospective dance partners and assessing their attractions.

As soon as the band struck up there was a surge of young men towards the girls.

Methods of requesting a female to dance varied. Some

44

gents simply touched the girl of their choice on the elbow and nodded towards the dance floor.

A more articulate man would utter the laconic invitation heard only in Glasgow dance halls – 'Ur ye furrup?' Usually the damsel nodded and meekly preceded her partner to the dance floor.

But sometimes a questing male would meet with a hostile reception. In such a case she would rebuff him with the stark intimation – 'Nut dancin''.

At times a gent's Terpsichorean prowess might be called into question and the young lady would say, 'A champ dancer, did ye say? He's a dampt chancer.'

Now the brightly-lit dance halls of yesteryear have vanished to be replaced by dozens of discotheques into which thousands of young people cram themselves nightly. Few middle-aged citizens visit these establishments.

But other forms of dancing are engaged in. In the summer all over Scotland there are Highland gatherings. At these, young girls wearing the kilt compete in Highland dancing contests.

On raised platforms and often in broiling sunshine they compete *en masse*. These anxious-faced aspirants hop and skip for hours through the intricacies of traditional Scottish dance.

Watching intently from the sidelines are their proud mothers. At one of these marathons I felt sorry for one exhausted-looking competitor who was egged on to Terpsichorean glory by her domineering mother. The drama went something like this:

MOTHER: (*Shouts*) Aw hivvins, will ye hurry up? Get
          a move on, wull ye?
          (*Dancer enters, teetering on bowed legs*

and carrying two swords.)
Whit's haudin' ye up?

DANCER: (*Tremulously*) Ah think it's ma legs . . .

MOTHER: Lissen, have you nae wish tae be a success at the Highland dancin'? Have ye nae culture aboot ye at a'? . . . Is this a' the thanks Ah get for givin' ye two quarters at the dancin' an' buyin' ye a' thae medals?

DANCER: (*Wails*) Ah'm TIRED Mammy! I don't waant tae dance!

MOTHER: Ye don't waant tae dance?! . . . Look, ma lass, you'll dance! Ye'll dance if it kills me!

DANCER: (*Terrified*) Yes, Mammy! I'll dance, Mammy!

MOTHER: I should think so! Get down those swords! (*Dancer puts down swords crossed. Mother switches on sword dance on transistor and dancer starts to dance half-heartedly with sulky expression, arms dangling at her side.*) Where are your arms?

DANCER: (*Stops and holds out dangling arms*) Here they are, Mammy. I've still got them, Mammy.

MOTHER: Oh would that no' scunner ye! . . . (*Shouts*) Get them up an' keep dancin'! (*She increases speed of transistor music and dancer tries in vain to keep up with it. She treads on the swords and comes to an untidy stop.*)

DANCER: Oh Mammy, I think I've cut ma wee toe!

MOTHER: Cut your wee toe? Is THAT a' ye've got tae complain aboot? Ye've got tae make SOME sacrifices, ye know. Ye're gonny beat that Morag McSwain if it's the last thing ye do! That Morag McSwain's beaten ye at every contest ye've been in! I'm sick o' her mother crawin' over me!

DANCER: I'm sorry, Mammy. (*Near tears*)

MOTHER: Never mind bein' sorry. You get on wi' yer practice . . .

DANCER: Mammy, can I go for a . . .

MOTHER: NO! . . . You're havin' no more ice-cream! . . . I'm goin' away for ma dinner noo. You keep dancin' till I come back. Get movin'! (*Dancer, looking very glum, starts to dance again.*)

MOTHER: Here, whit are ye lookin' like that for? Smile when ye're dancin'! Smile or I'll belt ye one!

DANCER: Yes, Mammy, I'll smile! (*Forced smile*)

MOTHER: Ye'll never beat Morag McSwain wi' a face like that. Jist you keep dancin' an' smilin'! (*Mother goes off. Dancer dances on briefly. Then she stops and puts out her tongue in the direction of her mother.*)

DANCER: I hate her! She's away to have a wee snack. Just one sangwidge – a loaf cut in two wi' two black puddins in it . . . And I hate Morag McSwain! She fancies herself, ye know. Calls herself the Fonteyn of Fintry . . . Mind ye, I've won a medal or two masel'. See this one . . . (*Indicates largest of tin medals.*) This is the one I got for the high jump at the Drumtochty Games. I didnae MEAN tae enter for the high jump. But before the dancin' started I went behind a hedge tae powder ma nose . . .

Naebody tell't me the field was full o' thistles. Oh an' this medal here. I got this yin for bravery. I was competin' against Morag McSwain at the Kilcheuchter Games. Well, I'd just started tae do ma sword dance. Suddenly I felt somethin' slippin'. The more I danced the further they slipped . . . Then I looked doon at the spectators and realised I'd been sabotaged! There was Morag McSwain laughin' up at me and wavin' a dauda elastic. Ma Mammy yelled tae me – 'Show yer initiative!' I yelled back – 'I'm tryin' *no*' tae!' There was nothing for it. I had to switch to the sailor's hornpipe.
(*Brief sailor's hornpipe with one hand on stomach and other behind back as if holding up knickers.*)
That was jist ONE disappointment. I was heartbroken at Braemar when I wasn't selected to dance before the Royal Family. Ye can guess who was picked – Morag McSwain. I was jist her understudy. Oh, I was mortificated! . . . Well, jist before she was due to dance she was found unconscious in a corner of the park – absolutely unconscious. So I took her place. Oh, I was that excited! . . . I didnae even notice I was dancin' wi' the lead pipe in ma hand. Ach but I'm sick o' this Highland dancin'. I was never meant to be . . .

MOTHER: (*Re-appearing*) Heh, you! Are you still practisin'?

DANCER: (*In terror*) Oh she's back!
MOTHER: I hope you havenae been standin' aboot
            daen' nothin'! If you're gonny be a dancin'
            star ye've got tae work at it!
DANCER: Yes, Mammy, I'll do that. I'll do whitever
            ye say.
MOTHER: (*Changing to cajolery*) Ye understand,
            Marilyn, don't ye? Mammy jist wants ye to
            be a success.
DANCER: Yes, Mammy.
MOTHER: Mammy jist wants her wee girlie to get
            more points from the judges, more points
            than Morag McSwain. When you win
            points it's like Mammy winning points.
DANCER: I see. Ye want a lot o' points, Mammy.
            (*Picks up swords.*)
MOTHER: That's right, dear!
DANCER: (*Suddenly pointing the swords at mother*)
            Well, here's a coupla points tae start wi'!
            (*She advances on mother who turns tail
            and flees.*)

7 Wigs, Wellies and Wallies

Many Glaswegians show an inordinate interest in other people's aids to appearance such as wigs, wellies (Wellington boots) and wallies (artificial teeth).

An individual who wears a hair-piece is regarded as being guilty of deception. This is hotly resented.

Of a wig-wearing woman it will be said, 'She waashes her herr every week an' hings it oot tae dry wi' the rest o' her waashin'.' And on wigs such a remark was heard: 'Maggie never suspected her boyfriend wore a wig until wan night she caressed his heid an' his herr came away in her haun'.'

Of a gent it was said, 'He's got a price on his heid. Naw, he's no' waantit by the polis. He peyed forty quid fur that herrpiece o' his.'

The producer of a summer show I was in had something of an obsession with wigs. Dissatisfied with one lady performer's hair he ordered that she should be given a wig before setting foot on the stage.

One evening he had to visit her in her dressing-room. The visit was a short one. He espied the wig lying on a chair on to which she'd tossed it.

He staggered from the room, deeply shocked. 'She's achieved the impossible!' he cried, 'She's got the wig looking even worse than her own hair!'

Women who, in all weathers, elect to wear Wellington boots, come in for some scathing criticism. Of one such wellie-wearer it may be said – 'She werrs thae wellies so's her legs'll no' look sae bowlly.'

Two ladies were discussing a diminutive neighbour when one disclosed, 'Wee Jenny was in terrible pain wi' her legs an' she was hardly able tae walk.'

'So Ah heard,' said the other, 'But Ah hear she's all right noo efter the operation.'

'Oh, whit kinna operation did she huv?'

'They cut three inches aff the tops o' her wellies.'

And so we come to that favourite subject of cynical comment, dentures, known as 'choppers' but usually 'wallies'.

A Polish Army officer who was stationed in Scotland during the war and with whom I was acquainted had a number of gold teeth. He told me he was puzzled by a remark he overheard a shopgirl making to a colleague. 'He's got a gub like Fort Knox,' she said. 'Aye,' said the second damsel, 'he's got that much gold in his mooth he's got tae sleep wi' his heid in a safe.'

There is the sad saga of the girl trumpet-player. 'She practises on her trumpet day an' night,' goes the tale. 'Her lips are that hard, every time she kisses her boyfriend she breks his wallies.'

A gent's artificial eye was the object of intense interest to his neighbours. 'Which wan's his glass eye?' asked one. 'The wan wi' the kindly expression,' was the reply.

Despite the warmth and kindliness of Glaswegians, it doesn't do to be over-sensitive in the city.

8 *Shop talk*

Shopping in Glasgow can be an entertaining adventure. Many shop assistants, especially the females, employ an engaging frankness in their dealings with customers.

The young ladies do not hesitate to guide customers to a wise expenditure of their cash.

A friend of mine who was about to purchase an expensive brand of after-shave lotion was advised: 'Don't buy it. It'll make ye stink like hell an' weemin hate it.'

A lady buying a hat also received candid advice from the maiden at the hat counter:

'Oh ye like that hat?' she asked, surprise mingled with disapproval. 'It certainly wouldn't be *my* choice. Ah aye think if ye're kinda full in the face ye shouldny wear a wee pillbox hat. It looks like a thimble on top o' a dumplin'.'

Some of these delightful shop assistants exhibit a certain dislike of their jobs. Here we see two such dissatisfied damsels, Clara and Rosalie, extremely disgruntled at being transferred from one department to another in a multiple store.

SCENE: (*Paperbacks department of big store, like one in Boots Ltd. Clara with feather duster in hand is standing behind a bank of paperbacks. She looks defiantly at the Manager who is addressing her.*)

MANAGER: Nonsense, Miss McClurg! ANYONE can sell paperbacks.

CLARA: But Ah don't waant tae sell paperbacks! Ma heart's in toilet assessories.

MANAGER: Come, come, this is the most important department in the store! What is everyone reading nowadays?

CLARA: Aboot Joan Collins's latest marriage.

MANAGER: Exactly! Not at all! Everybody's reading paperbacks! Look at that – history, drama, romance! What more could anyone want?

CLARA: Toilet assessories.

MANAGER: That'll do! Now listen, here are your instructions. First of all, I want you to push *The Wayward Bus*.

CLARA: . . . Ye waant me tae WHIT?

MANAGER: Push *The Wayward Bus*.

CLARA: Away an' push it yersel'!

MANAGER: And furthermore, I'm giving you six dozen Corgis to get rid of.

CLARA:	Oh for Hivvin's sake! He wants me tae droon dugs nixt!
MANAGER:	No! No! NO! . . . Oh, carry on with the work!
	(*He exits.*)
CLARA:	Paperbacks! . . . Dampt liberty! . . . (*Picks up book.*) Whit's this? *Hollywid Husbands* Oh, wid ye credit that! (*Turns page rapidly.*) Oh my! (*Reads.*) 'His mouth sought hers. She felt his searing breath on her . . . (*Turns page feverishly*) . . . 'bare minimum and even that was too much for Rodney' . . . Here, that canny be right. Oh my, the pages is jine't thegither! Wherra perra scissors? (*Rosalie enters.*)
ROSALIE:	Haw, Clerra!
CLARA:	(*Hiding book hastily under counter*) Eh? . . . Oh hullo! What are YOU doin' here?
ROSALIE:	Ah've been shiftit!
CLARA:	Shiftit?
ROSALIE:	Aye, the man tell't me he wiz transferrin' me tae 'books' . . . Ah thought he sayed Ah wiz GETTIN' ma books.
CLARA:	Oh, transferred. That's a sin, Rosalie. Ye were that happy at the dug food counter.
ROSALIE:	Ah know. Ah got sich a shock Ah hud tae take a coupla Boab Martin's. (*Enter young man who browses.*)
CLARA:	Aw well, Ah'll help ye. Ye see, there's aye been books in oor family.
ROSALIE:	HUZ there, Clerra?

CLARA:	Aye . . . Ah'm gaun' wi' a bookie's runner, ma feyther's aye gettin' his books an' ma grannie's been booked for breach o' the peace.
ROSALIE:	But Clerra, Ah've never read a book.
CLARA:	Ach, don't worry, hen. Ye never ett dug biscuits but ye were a' right at the dug food counter.
ROSALIE:	But Ah DID eat dug biscuits.
CLARA:	Well, there ye are, well . . . Here, this'll interest ye. (*Shows Rosalie* Hollywood Husbands. *They both look, gape, giggle and nudge one another. Business man enters. Girls don't notice him.*)
B.MAN:	I say, have you any Penguins?
CLARA:	(*Still engrossed in book*) Second counter on the left.
B.MAN:	For PENGUINS?
CLARA:	Aye, that's right.
B.MAN:	(*Bewildered*) Thank you. (*Drifts off.*)
CLARA:	Imagine askin' US fur choaclit biscuits! (*Young man, reading book, begins to snicker.*)
ROSALIE:	Whit's he laughin' at, Clerra?
CLARA:	Ach, just a heidcase. Where were we? (*They resume* Hollywood Husbands.)
ROSALIE:	Oh, look at that bit! . . . Could ye imagine Big Sanny sayin' that tae YOU?
CLARA:	(*Grimly*) He'd get wan on the jaw if he did.
ROSALIE:	What does he mean by 'cohabit'?
CLARA:	Ah'm no' sure, but Ah think he means business.

58

(*Woman enters briskly.*)

WOMAN: Look here, can you supply me with *Love in the South Seas*?

CLARA: Naw, missus, this is 'Books' no' 'Cook's'.

WOMAN: What are you talking about? (*To Rosalie*) Do YOU have *Love in the South Seas*?

ROSALIE: Naw, Ah never go further than Roathesay.

WOMAN: Oh, *really*?

CLARA: Jist a minnit, is it a nuvvel ye want?

WOMAN: No, it's non-fiction.

CLARA: Oh, we don't stock that kinna stuff.

WOMAN: (*Pointing*) But haven't you got *The Life of Nelson*?

CLARA: No, we huvny got the life o' a dug.

ROSALIE: (*Who has picked up* Hollywood Husbands) Oh my!

WOMAN: (*Grabs at book*) Oh, for goodness sake, I'll take that one.

CLARA: (*Snatches book from Rosalie*) Ye will nutt! I'm takin' this one hame . . . Ye know, Rosalie, I'm beginnin' tae enjoy this job.

WOMAN: I can't imagine how you got this job. What do YOU know about any great works?

CLARA: Plenty! I was two years in Buchanan's sweetie works.

WOMAN: Oh, good day! (*Flounces off.*)

CLARA: Cheery-bye . . . Ignurint bizzim that. Ye can see it in her face.

(*Young man, reading, laughs. Clara and*

	Rosalie study him for a few seconds with interest.)
ROSALIE:	He seems tae be enjoyin' himsel'.
CLARA:	He's away wi' the burds, that yin. (*Old rake enters. He beckons secretively to Rosalie.*)
OLD RAKE:	Excuse me!
ROSALIE:	*Me?* (*Old rake nods. She approaches him warily.*)
OLD RAKE:	Is *Lady Chatterley's Lover* in yet?
ROSALIE:	I don't know. Whit does he look like?
OLD RAKE:	No, no . . . I'm after *Lady Chatterley's Lover.*
ROSALIE:	Oh, ur ye?
CLARA:	(*Digs her in the back*) 'Sup wi' Auld Spice?
ROSALIE:	Oh Clerra, this is Lord Chatterley. He's waantin' tae get a haud o' his wife's fancy man!
CLARA:	'Zat so? Well, he's no' gettin' a haud o' him in here! Oot ye go, mister. This is a respectable paperback shop.
OLD RAKE:	(*Looks at books*) Good gracious, be quiet, girl! Ah, a cheap edition of *The Surgeon's Log.* (*Picks up book and turns to the back.*) Have they taken out the appendix?
CLARA:	Ye better ask the surgeon . . . Three quid. (*Old rake pays up, takes book and goes off. Posh woman enters.*)
P.WOMAN:	(*To Rosalie*) I want something for my bedside . . . It's a Great Pan.

ROSALIE:	Oh, the hardware department's on the ground floor.
P.WOMAN:	No, no, it's one of those mysteries.
CLARA:	It's a mystery a' right.
P.WOMAN:	Oh surely *you* know what I mean. Aren't you familiar with Mickey Spillane?
CLARA:	Oh, I've never met the man in my life! Whit an insult! Get oota here before Ah send for the polis!
P.WOMAN:	But I simply asked for . . .
CLARA:	Ye're askin' fur trouble! (*Raises Hollywood Husbands.*) . . . Oot ye go before Ah gie ye *Hollywid Husbands* straight oan the face!
P.WOMAN:	I'm going to get the manager!
CLARA:	Get who ye like . . . (*Young man laughs into book.*) Whit are YOU laughin' at? Gimme that book! (*Snatches book from young man.*) That'll be £4.95p.
Y.MAN:	£4.95p? What for?
CLARA:	Ye've read half the book. Oh, therr cheek fur ye! He's got a bus ticket in it tae keep the place! (*Young man recoils, Rosalie takes book and looks at title.*)
ROSALIE:	Oh, Clerra, there's a mistake in this book!
CLARA:	(*Looking at book*) Oh, so there is! Oh, that's shockin'! (*Manager strides in angrily followed by posh woman.*)
CLARA:	Here, there's a terrible mistake in this book. It says – *Gone With The Wind* by Margaret Mitchell.

MANAGER: (*Breathing fire*) Oh, and what should it be?

CLARA: Margaret Thatcher.

9 *The Tintock Cup*

As a youngster I remember pantomimes in Glasgow fell into two distinct categories, the ones presented by Tom Arnold at the Alhambra and Howard & Wyndham at the Theatre Royal, and the very different sort to be found at the Queens, the Empress, Pavilion and the Princess's.

The posh ones disdained Scottish comedians in those days. It was Dorothy Ward and Douglas Byng and pink teacups passed along at the interval. Sammy Murray reigned at the Queens and fought a constant battle with the Watch Committee on his bluer material. Gags would be ordered out – only to slip in a couple of nights later. Adventurous West-Enders would go 'slumming' to the Queens, a great favourite with male 'Varsity students.

The Princess's was the favourite though, for all Glaswegians. They crossed the Clyde in droves to see what new nonsense Harry McKelvie had dreamed up for them in the Gorbals. It was never a traditional panto subject, and was characterised by a 13-letter title – usually the comic's panto name Tammy Tummshie or the like.

By 1949 the old Princess's had for several years been the Citizen's Theatre – the brainchild of the Scottish playwright James Bridie. It is said that when Harry McKelvie (who had leased his theatre on very moderate terms to the Citizens) saw the first production, he bitterly regretted his generosity. He had been given to understand that he was playing godfather to a true Scottish national theatre – an Abbey of the Gorbals.

For a while – too short a while – it did become just that, but it was perhaps unfortunate that their first production in the newly-acquired theatre was 'Johnson over Jordan', Priestley's essay into the German Expressionist theatre. McKelvie probably never forgave Bridie, and perhaps as a posthumous gesture of repentance Bridie decided in 1949 to stage a McKelvie-type panto in the old McKelvie theatre. Bridie handed us a huge panto 'book' – but gave us *carte blanche* to edit and interpolate stuff of our own. He called it 'The Tintock Cup' – preserving the 13-letter tradition.

John Casson, knowing of my troup entertainments background, summoned me to be his assistant producer and everybody in the company started to pitch in with ideas. Duncan Macrae knew of someone called Alex Mitchell and Alex and almost every member of the company contributed something. The result was even madder than McKelvie's pantos in their heyday. Because the story mattered even less than in traditional pantos I

got the idea of losing the story completely during the last four items before the finale.

I reckoned that comedy *could* follow comedy provided we went from dancing comedy to patter comedy to singing comedy and back to patter. The idea was to give the audience no time to recover equilibrium – to induce hysteria by not letting up on the laughs. To say it worked is an understatement. Its incredible success changed the face of Scottish comedy and ever after all Scottish pantos boasted native comedians.

Macrae was signed for the Alhambra the following year and two years later I was signed by Howard & Wyndham. Memories of 'The Tintock Cup' are legion but I have a special affection for two items I wasn't in: Alex Mitchell's 'Hing' with Macrae and James Gibson and Molly Urquhart as 'Tatty Bacchante'.

I wrote this piece for Molly and she delivered it with consumate skill. Lights came up to reveal her ample form in leopard skin, a laurel wreath on bedraggled hair and a bunch of grapes held like Nightingale's lamp beside her right eye. She then launched into:

I'm Tatty Bacchante – I'm everyone's auntie,
The darling of all who love beer.
I eat grapes by the dozen and look like that cousin
That turns up blind drunk at New Year.
Oh I used to get toasted in Athens and Rome,
And senators fought to see who'd take me home,
In those days the men blew the beer off the foam –
Tatty Bacchante's yer auntie,
Spare a wee hauf at New Year.

I'm Tatty Bacchante – I'm everyone's auntie,
The fresh word for 'out on the skite'.

Every new tax on liquor has made me feel sicker,
They're ruining ma Setterday night.
In the blackout I had a great time with a Pole,
But now that exporting our whisky's the goal,
It's New York for me or I'm back on the dole –
Tatty Bacchante's yer auntie,
Spare a wee hauf at New Year.

I'm Tatty Bacchante – I'm everyone's auntie,
The Priestess of Pimms Number One.
Though I look a tough heathen – no kiddin' I'm freezin',
A leopard skin isnal aw fun!
A Hollywood goddess can turn up in mink
And tipple till all hours – it does make ye think,
The nine thirty closing will drive me to drink –
Tatty Bacchante's yer auntie,
Spare a wee hauf at New Year.

I'm Tatty Bacchante – I'm everyone's auntie,
The bosom companion of Zeus.
I suppose it was fate that the plasterer's mate
Got too plastered to finish oor hoose.
Bacchanalian orgies and nights on the spree
Are exempted from tax for Miss Vivien Leigh,
I wish the Arts Council would just sponsor me –
Tatty Bacchante's yer auntie,
Spare a wee hauf at New Year.

I'm Tatty Bacchante – I'm everyone's auntie,
Except for the man that's T.T.
With some tax off the wine we can have a rare time,
Come up any time and see me.
If you'll just name the place where you'd like us to meet,
As long as it's licenced my day is complete,

Though you may have to cart me to Sauchiehall Street –
Tatty Bacchante's yer auntie,
Spare a wee hauf at New Year.

It is hardly surprising that some of the most apposite lines have dated – but the memory of Molly reaching higher and higher in volume as she backcourt–sang the concluding two lines of each stanza is timeless.

10 *Theatricalities*

The Graveyard of English Comics was the description bestowed on the large Empire Theatre that stood at the Eastern end of Sauchiehall Street. Its audiences, especially on Friday evenings, were noted for the vociferous and angry reception accorded to performers from south of the Border.

The rumpus was not unlike that heard in a radio broadcast from the House of Commons during a particularly stormy debate.

Even those experienced comedy troupers Morecambe and Wise were disconcerted by the rowdiness of an Empire audience.

The singer/comedian Des O'Connor was so startled by the uproar that greeted his appearance that he fell in a faint as soon as he set foot on the stage.

The conductor of the pit orchestra leaned forward over the footlights and called to the prostrate figure, 'Is this part of the act?' The audience were so surprised that they became quiet and Des recovered and won them over completely.

Another English artiste, a male impersonator making one of several farewell appearances, also met with hostile uproar as soon as she appeared.

But she had a gallant champion. A tall gent rose from his seat in the front row of the stalls and faced the howling mob.

'Aw, come on,' he appealed to them. 'Gi'e the poor aul' coo a chance.'

This unexpected intervention brought a brief period of silence during during which the lady artiste walked to the footlights and rebuked the noisy mob with the heartfelt words, 'Thank goodness there's ONE gentleman in the audience.'

Performers in some of the smaller theatres faced various types of ordeal.

One old-time comedian told me of arriving at a small theatre in Argyle Street and noticing patrons entering with large paper bags. In a matter-of-fact way the manager told the comic, 'They've been to the fruit market for their ammunition.'

The comic and his partner soon discovered the significance of this disclosure when during their act one of their cracks didn't appeal to the audience and the hapless artistes were bombarded with a selection of fruit and vegetables that were far from fresh.

Regular performers at the theatre regarded such demonstrations as something to be endured philosophically and became experts at dodging the putrifying missiles.

In the smaller theatres also, performers who incurred

the audience's displeasure were subjected to such insults as 'Away an' work,' 'Away an' get waashed', or simply, 'Pit him aff'.

Comedians sometimes made fun of their fellow performers. Singers were favourite victims and often heard were fake announcements such as 'Miss Blank will now sing that touching ballad "You May Have a Bleeding Heart, But I've Got a Floating Kidney"', or 'Your favourite tenor is now going to sing for you that lovely old number "Father, Take Your Feet Off the Table and Give the Cheese a Chance"'.

The poignant story of a girl singer was told me by a veteran Glasgow theatre-goer. It seems that in a small theatre she made the mistake of singing an operatic aria. This was not appreciated by the audience and the applause at the end of the song was, to say the least, perfunctory.

The singer, a lady-like and demure-looking damsel, looked down at the audience, brushed a tear from her eye, walked down to the front of the stage and addressed the audience with the words 'Ya sho'er o' ignurint bastards'.

Alas, only three theatres remain in Glasgow. I am happy to report that their audiences are generally appreciative and invariably well-behaved.

11 *The man they called Mr Glasgow*

Glasgow has always been fortunate in having a plentiful supply of native comedians, the men who reap a rich harvest of fun from the idiosyncrasies of their fellow citizens, male and female.

Heading the current drove of drolls is Billy Connolly, the only bearded comedian in the city's theatrical history. A gifted raconteur and a keen observer of the lower strata of Glasgow life. Now based in London, he has become something of a cult figure there.

Andy Cameron has an immense fund of Glaswegian-accented jokes which he tells with superb skill.

But if I had to choose the best ever exponent of down-to-earth Glasgow humour, I would nominate the late and great Tommy Morgan.

The title 'Mr Glasgow' fitted him exactly.

He was born in Bridgeton and the family didn't have much money. As a schoolboy Tommy helped out by delivering morning rolls.

'Ah aye saw that ma Maw got plenty of them,' he told me. 'The family lived on thae rolls – till the baker found oot an' sacked me.'

When eventually he was in the big money he often looked back on the poverty-stricken days of his childhood.

He told me how he borrowed an old overcoat from a pal in order to emigrate to the States. He was to send back the money for it when he got a job in New York.

But Tommy changed his mind about emigrating. He was wearing the coat at Bridgeton Cross one winter's day when he saw its owner approaching.

'Aw, so ye didnae go tae the States efter a'?' said the overcoat owner. 'See's back ma bliddy coat!'

He wrenched it off Tommy's back and went off with it, muttering angrily, 'Bloomin' fly man!'

When only sixteen in 1916 Tommy volunteered for the Army. His family went to Central Station, Glasgow, to see him off to the battlefront.

But when the train stopped five minutes later at Eglinton Street station the boy-soldier became homesick.

The carriage door was locked but he climbed out of the window and made his way back to Bridgeton.

When his father and tearful mother got home they were amazed to see Tommy sitting at the fireside.

'Whit are ye daen' here?' shouted his father angrily. 'Get back tae the sojers!' And he gave the reluctant warrior a cuff on the ear.

Back went Tommy to spend his seventeenth birthday under fire in a Flanders dug-out.

When I first met Tommy the thin little Bridgeton lad had grown into a tall well-fed-looking man who was making something like £300 a week, big money for a star in those days.

Morgan's face and voice helped him to fame and fortune.

The face was round – 'big bawface' was his own description of it – and the blue eyes could express fierce resentment or great pleasure most eloquently.

The voice was unforgettable – loud, rasping and unmistakably Glasgow. It sounded as if he had a perpetually sore throat.

Tommy Morgan's career began when he won a prize in a go-as-you-please competition, one of those talent contests that were held in little halls throughout Glasgow fifty years ago.

Then he became feed to comedian Tommy York. Amongst their one-night engagements was one at the tiny Panoptican Theatre (later a cinema) in Argyle Street, Glasgow.

'I mind the surprise I got when York an' me played the Gaiety, Leith, for the first time,' Tommy recounted.

'Naebody threw anything at us – and we were used to being pelted in the wee Glasgow theatres we played.'

Eventually Morgan became the comic and York his feed.

The Morgan Summer Show ran for fourteen successive years at the Pavilion Theatre, Glasgow.

Tommy put on the package show, engaging the artistes and receiving salary and a percentage of the gross drawings out of which he payed his company.

In the theatre his word was law and he was known as 'The Guv'nor'.

He rehearsed his own sketches. He never revealed what

his own lines were but his clutch of feeds had to take down their lines in jotters.

Heaven help the feed who forgot his lines during a performance. 'Ah can mind MA lines – an' Ah've nae jotter,' Tommy would say in front of the audience.

One young man in the company committed the unforgivable sin. He ad-libbed during a sketch.

Tommy recoiled from him as if stung. 'Okay!' he cried, 'YOU be the coamic!' Then he slammed down his big comic's bunnet on the wretched youth's head.

Morgan constantly ad-libbed at members of the company and the audience.

For a time his favourite butt was a wee woman in the company who appeared in many of his sketches.

She was an abstemious lady but Tommy would tell the audience that she'd just come from Lauder's Bar next door or that she was 'never oot the Atholl Arms'.

When she made play with a lorgnette in one sketch he cried 'Glesses at the end o' a stick! She'd rather stick at the end o' a gless.'

He could be quite crushing if annoyed.

I remember one brash young artiste asking him for a rise. 'You get plenty but I'm just paid in sweeties,' the young man told The Guv'nor.

'Is that so?' said Tommy in a deceptively calm tone.

'I want more money,' was the reply.

'Oh well, ye'll get more money,' The Guv'nor assured him, 'Just go to the manager and he'll give ye a fortnight's wages . . . Then ye're OOT!'

One year Morgan did an unheard-of thing for a Scots comedian. He paid a composer money to have an opening chorus written for the show.

The piece of music turned out to be very short and the composer's fee very stiff – sixty-six pounds.

Tommy paid up. 'I gave him merr notes than he gave me,' he told me ruefully.

He was very interested in his own native Glesca patter. He pointed out to me that lots of Glasgow folk never use the 'th' sound.

He gave the example of 'murra an' farra' for 'mother and father'.

One day as we walked down Renfield Street he stopped, quite excited. 'Did you hear that?' he cried. 'That lassie said to her chum "Wherr urrey?" an' hur pal said "Errur owrerr".'

Then thoughtfully he added – 'I'll have tae dae mair walkin' an' listenin' tae keep up wi' the patter.'

The Morgan lifestyle was rather extravagant at times, a kind of backlash from his young days.

He relished having a Rolls-Bentley with chauffeur, luxury flat in the West End of Glasgow and, of course, his many expensive suits.

He entertained in the best restaurants, paying the bill from a large roll of notes he invariably carried in his right trouser pocket.

He arranged to take the film star, Caesar Romero, to lunch at the posh One-O-One Restaurant.

At the Pavilion stage door Romero was halted by a stage-hand who'd been in Hollywood and wanted to chat.

Romero good-humouredly chatted with the man and Tommy walked on down Renfield Street. Then, greatly impatient at being kept waiting, he wheeled round and shouted – 'Come oan, Caesar! We'll never get tae the Wan-O-Wan the day!'

In London Tommy usually ate at the Savoy Grill. It was there, *en route* to Cannes, that he startled and mystified the head waiter by calling – 'Is ma dinner no' up yit? Ah've an airyplane tae Cans tae catch!'

I remember him telling me he was going on holiday to Nice. 'That'll be nice,' I said.

'Naw, naw!' he said pityingly. 'Ye don't pronounce it "nice". It's "niece", ye know, yer sister's wean.'

But he never got to Nice. He'd almost reached his destination in the Rolls-Bentley when he switched on the car radio.

From it came an excited commentary on a Celtic game.

It was too much for him. 'Turn the car roon'!' he told his chauffeur. 'We're gaun' hame. Ah must see the Celtic play Rangers.'

But Tommy could laugh at himself for liking the high life.

I once asked him for his favourite joke.

Without hesitation he said – 'It's one I've never cracked on the stage. It' aboot a poor aul' tramp at two in the mornin' standin' ootside Glasgow City Chambers where a big charity ball's goin' on.

'Suddenly a debutante wi' a mink coat an' hingin' wi' diamonds comes oot an' starts tae cross tae a big Rolls-Royce standin' at the kerb.

'The aul' tramp goes up tae this posh lassie. "Can ye give me a shillin' so's I can get a bed fur the night?" he says.

'The debutante looks doon at him, flamin' mad. "How DARE you ask me for money?" she snaps. "Don't you realise that I've been dancing for you and your kind all night?"'

Unlike the debutante, Tommy was generous. Many an artiste down on his luck got a hand-out from him . . . and he dreaded anyone discovering he was a benefactor.

Towards the end of his career he was desperately ill. But he struggled on in his summer show.

People, as always, flocked to see him and enjoy his gutsy Glasgow humour.

But, after a courageous battle against pain and weakness, he had to give up.

A few months later he died – almost penniless. The high life, the odd big bet on a horse, medical bills, the loans he made to people . . . possibly these ran away with much of his money.

I can still hear that gallus, rasping voice with its rich authentic Glasgow patter.

And so can many folk to whom Tommy Morgan brought many evenings of laughter.

12   Mr Ballhead

A brilliant Scottish comedian never achieved great fame. He didn't want it. He was Willie McCulloch, now remembered fondly only by those in their seventies and eighties. McCulloch, a self-effacing genius, wouldn't give up his Civil Service job to become a professional entertainer. He was the first man I know of to commit Glasgow humour to paper.

He delivered his comic monologues mainly at smoking concerts, never in theatres. I possess some of the gramophone records he made. Out of his varied gallery of characters, my favourite is a pompous little Glasgow man, a know-all who, with supreme self-confidence and many malapropisms, delivers speeches at sundry functions.

McCulloch has him as Chairman of the Bridgeton Dramatic and Debating Society, announcing with some uncertainty over Roman numerals, 'the programme is dividit into two parts – Part Wan an' Part Eleven'.

This character so appealed to me that I appropriated him for my own use and called him Mr Ballhead, putting him into a number of different situations.

The following piece shows him as an eminent television newsreader being interviewed on his career.

INTERVIEWER:	John Ballhead, you are one of Britain's best-known newsreaders, perhaps even better known than Alistair Burnet and Sandy Gall. Your face and voice are familiar to millions of people. I'm wondering – how does one start being a newsreader? Do you have to have an honours degree in English or does training as an actor enable you to enunciate so clearly that every word you utter is understood by the listener?
BALLHEAD:	Well ackchally, A' rem things is of paranoid importance in a joab like mines. Us newsreaders has reelly got to have unpeccable diction. So correc' enounciation is a preperquisite for us.
INTERVIEWER:	I take it that your vowel sounds must be limpid. I mean, you must keep your vowels open.
BALLHEAD:	Undubitably. I never partake of a refreshment before a broadcast.

84

INTERVIEWER:	No doubt you will have to watch your consonants. Am I right in saying that you can have no glottal stops?
BALLHEAD:	Quite ri'. When I patter away it's a matter of clarity. It's better I utter the words with no stutterin' or mutterin'.
INTERVIEWER:	I understand that you read the news from a machine, an auto-cue. Does this mean that you have to be an expert in sight-reading?
BALLHEAD:	Oh definitely. The Director General hisself was impressed by my sight-reading. He said, 'Look at that sight reading!'
INTERVIEWER:	How exactly did you come to join the BBC?
BALLHEAD:	That event came about in a most fortuatitious manner. You see, before becoming a newsreader I used to yell out the news.
INTERVIEWER:	You YELLED out the news?
BALLHEAD:	Precisely . . . at the corner of Union Street and Argyle Street. At that busy juncture you could hear me yelling 'Times, r'Express, Daily Wrecker . . .' There was times when I called out such news items as – 'Heatwave in the Gorbals' and 'Glasga Murdur – Wumman Chokes her Sink.'
INTERVIEWER:	But how did that lead to your

	becoming a television newsreader?
BALLHEAD:	Well, one evening as I was waring out my . . . er . . . bawling out my wares, a BBC executive drew up in his Porsche. He was on his way from Blythswood Square and he stopped with such suddenness that the young lady with him almost precipiatatit her napper through the windscreen. The BBC executive was excited at the sound of my voice. 'Never,' he said, 'have I saw such vocal virtuosity!'
INTERVIEWER:	It was your newspaper-selling technique that impressed him? Your loud bawling . . .
BALLHEAD:	Yes, it was all bawls. It seemed the timber of my voice appealed to him and in no time at all he wheeched me up to the BBC Headquarters in Glasgow. My career as a TV personality had commenced.
INTERVIEWER:	But it wasn't long before you were lured south to read the BBC news from London.
BALLHEAD:	No, it wasn't long. But, before that, I had underwent a course in paper-shuffling.
INTERVIEWER:	Paper-shuffling?
BALLHEAD:	Yes, you know how newsreaders fold up sundry dauds of paper

86

after they have finished a bulletin. Well, I passed the paper-shuffling test with such consummated ease that the BBC examiners were completely astounderated. My experience as a newsboy was responsible for this uncanny dexterity of mines. So I joined Sue Lawley and Jan Leeming.

INTERVIEWER: Don't you work in a different way from them?

BALLHEAD: Entirely different. Due to my literry expertyse I was permitted to write my own texts.

INTERVIEWER: Well, we have some clips of your broadcasts and the first one shows you making a very important announcement. (*Clip*)

BALLHEAD) In the House of Commons today a decision that will affect the lifes of innumerable people was took. Permission was gave to the BBC to set up a Fifth Television Channel. It will have only two performers who, each day, will work a twelve-hour shift. This will enable the public to see more of Terry Wogan. The announcement was intimidated to the house by the newly-appointed Minister for the Arts, the Right Honourable William Connolly. He also announced that the TV

	licence fee will be raised to £194. This will insure that the services of the two performers will be exclusive to the . . . (*fade out*). (*End clip*)
INTERVIEWER:	A vital decision indeed . . . Mr Ballhead, I have often wondered why newsreaders never receive quite the adulation that is accorded pop singers, actors and actresses and even some comedians. Do you find it strange that you, for instance, never receive the star treatment?
BALLHEAD:	It is interesting that you should bring up that point. As a matter of fact, I went back to Glasgow after succeeding Mr Jimmy Boyle as Lord Rector of the University. After making my inaugurative address I was mobbed by a most vocifurous crowd.
INTERVIEWER:	Ah, they wanted to show their appreciation of your talent . . .
BALLHEAD:	Naw, they wanted to lynch me.
INTERVIEWER:	How remarkable . . . It's well known, of course, that you have a unique relationship with the Royal Family. I believe this is due to your discreet coverage of recent romantic events concerning Prince Andrew.
BALLHEAD:	Quite true. I think I may reveal that the Palace was not unpleased

at my discreetness about Andrew and that nice wee bit of stuff. No doubt that is why I appeared in the Honours List and was awardit the RBC.

INTERVIEWER: RBC? I haven't heard of that honour. I take it RBC stands for Royal Broadcasting Commendation.

BALLHEAD: No, Right Bliddy Crawler.

INTERVIEWER: Let's now have a look at your technique in covering the latest Royal romance.

(*Film clip*)

BALLHEAD: With my feet like lumps of leid, I am standing outside Cartford Hall, one of Britain's great historic piles. It is the domiacile of nobody more nor less than Her Graciousness the Duchess of Cartford, the mother of Lady Marinella Cartford who, it is said, may become the financee of the Prince. Lady Marinella has just went into the mansion after returning from the Special Unit at Barlinnie where she teaches a class in advanced crochet. I expect her to emerge out of the mansion at any moment and I hope to have a word with her . . .

(*Turns to look towards door of mansion*)

. . . She's not coming out so far

. . . Well . . . er . . . Lady
Marinella and the Prince have
been winching for some time now
but neethur him nor her has let
bug about it. She is very shy and
nobody could be more ladyliker
than hur. She does not like
publicity but she likes horses and
Corgi dugs. So, unvariably, she is
welcome at Buckingham Palace,
Windsor, Sandringham, Balmoral
and other Royal pads . . .
(*Looks anxiously again at door of
mansion*)
We're expecting her out here at
any moment now . . . No sign of
her yet . . . The Prince and hur
share an interest in culture and I
am informed that hur and hur
Royal lumbur may be setting out
to attend a recording of the
Tartan Terror programme. So I
expect that Lady Marinella will
. . . Ah, here she comes now!
(*Lady Marinella emerges from
mansion, head down and wearing
a floppy hat. Ballhead confronts
her, thrusting forward
hand-mike*)
Your Ladyship, I wonder if you
would be good enough for
to . . .

LADY M: (*Revealing face*) Aw beat it, ya
lousy wee ratbag! Get tae hell oot

ma road or Ah'll belt the bliddy
dial aff ye!
(*Fade out*)
(*End film clip*)

INTERVIEWER: Let's turn to another important aspect of your work. With your long experience as a television interviewer you acquired a deep knowledge of politics in different spheres.

BALLHEAD: Yes, I found that many politicians were talking a lot of spheres.

INTERVIEWER: Your interview with one particular union leader has been described as a masterly piece of political reporting. I think we have a clip of it . . . Yes, we have.

(*Clip*)

BALLHEAD: . . . Earlier I interviewed the leader of the union on the crisis that has arose in the Party . . . Mr Jerkins, has not the new way of electing a Prime Minister gave rise to some perturbulation among your members?

JERKINS: No, no, not at all. We may have had a few slight differences, but, after all, we are a democratic body and we are entitled to disagree in a democratic way, are we not? But if conference had rescinded the decision on Clause 8 of the constitution rules where

	would that have left us? I ask you – where?
BALLHEAD:	Er . . . with a certain distension in your ranks?
JERKINS:	No, no, no, no! Your question is a purely hypothetical one, purely hypothetical. Don't you see that if the block votes had gone to the constituency committees for ratification the situation would never have arisen? I put this to Neil *and* Roy and they agreed with me categorically, quite categorically.
BALLHEAD:	Did they? But what about Tony Benn?
JERKINS:	Now you are drawing a red herring across our discussion. What I want to stress to you is that, providing the majority decision of conference is valid, then my union would have to consider what their position was.
BALLHEAD:	Well, thank you very much for expressing your union's opinion.
JERKINS:	No, no, no, no! It wasn't my union's opinion I was expressing. I would have to go back to my executive for that. I was simply trying to convey to you the fact that the card vote of my members would have to be taken into . . .
BALLHEAD:	Aw shut yur face!
	(*End clip*)

INTERVIEWER:	Now, I don't know if you will agree with me, Mr Ballhead, but I think the most moving of your broadcasts came when you had to announce the grave illness of Queen N'Kimba of Bubuland.
BALLHEAD:	Indeed, never was I more greatly moved when I found that it had fell to me to record the misfortune that had ascended on that great queen and her people.
INTERVIEWER:	Well, let's see a clip of that memorable broadcast. *(Clip)*
BALLHEAD:	I had the good fortune to be present when Queen N'Kimba paid a state visit to London. It was a most suspicious occasion. There sat the regal black monarch in the royal coach, waving to the crowds. In front of her in the coach was a small black boy. He, I was informed, was to be her afternoon snack. Her Majesty was extremely fond of her chuck. Indeed, it was after a state banquet at her court in Bubuland that the dusky ninety-eight-year-old queen became undisposed. She had partook of a hearty meal of breadfruit, whulks and roast missionary garnished with sheep's eyeballs and the bitter fruit of the

zoomba tree. After it she had to be helped on to the throne, and it was there that she uttered, in her native tongue, the frightening words – 'Me ferr stappit'.

The Royal physicians were summoned and the Imperial stomach pump was brung into play. The fight to save Queen N'Kimba had began. From President Reagan came ten crates of jelly beans and 167 braces of peasants arrived from Sandringham. But it was not to no avail. The condition of the great intellectual and unlightened queen has gradually became worser. She has been unable to watch her favourite TV programme, *EastEnders*. The first bulletin to be received bore the momentious words which I have translated from the Bubuland language – 'Her Majesty has now became exceedingly peelly-wally.' . . . And so the life of this gracious monarch is proceeding to its termination.

Throughout this sad and historical evening medical bulletins have been issued regular every hour. The first, at 8.10 p.m. stated, 'Loud rumbling is emanuating from the royal

stomach and is causing considerable apprehensiveness.' The second, received at 9.10 p.m., gave the sinister news – 'The Queen's condition is extremely flatulent and her doctors are getting the wind up.' At 10.10 p.m. came the most gravest of the bulletins – 'Queen N'Kimba is slipping away.'
(*A sheet of paper is slipped in front of him*)
I regret for to inform youse that this is the last and final communication concerning the Queen – 'Tonight the natives of Bubuland are groaning in anguish, slabbering soot on their faces and tearing their hair out . . .'

In other words she's gettin' better!

13 *Parliamo Glasgow*

Alex and I were watching with great interest one instalment of a television series giving instruction in the Italian language.

This particular instalment showed a man and girl in a post office speaking Italian and buying stamps, postal orders and other articles. The sketch was then re-enacted, the players speaking the lines in carefully-enunciated English.

It then occurred to us that a similar method could be used to teach the Glasgow language. And so we evolved the *Parliamo Glasgow* series.

In the following sample, a mother and daughter are in a boutique. The daughter, helped by her mother, is buying a skirt in the fashion of the day known as a 'ra-ra'.

A lecturer is present to explain the niceties of the language.

LECTURER: This lesson concerns a young lady called Shona. Wishing to purchase a dress, she visits a boutique with her mother. We call this lesson . . .
SHONABYNAFROACK
Her mother disapproves of the low-cut dress her daughter is trying on. She hints that Shona is aspiring to appear on Page 3 of the *Daily Mirror*. So she subtly alters the meaning of her name by placing it in the middle of two other Glasgow words. She hisses . . .
YURSHONALOATABOADI
Shona resents this criticism and informs her mother that her boyfriend, Roddy, admired her physique. She declares proudly . . .
ROADIHINKSALOATAMABOADI
The mother does not wish to hear this. She regards with disfavour the young gentleman her daughter desires to impress. She condemns him with . . .
ROADIULNOTAKIZHONZAFYUR-BOADI
Shona ignores this allegation. She is still having difficulty in deciding what to buy. Eventually she catches sight of a short skirt and asks the shop assistant . . .
ZARRARARA?
The shopgirl confirms that it is a ra-ra skirt but doesn't think it would suit her.

Shona demands to know . . .
WHISSAMARRAWIRARARA?
The mother gets wind of the shop
assistant's objection and states . . .
FART
AGARRARARARAZFARTOONARRA
Shona, however, persists in trying on the
skirt. As the buxom damsel struggles to
pull it on the shop assistant makes the
urgent appeal . . .
NAEFARRAYILTERRARARA
Meanwhile the mother has espied a
collection of ladies' slacks and asks her
daughter . . .
JIKERRFURRAPERRAREMRERR?
She claims . . .
APERRAREMRERRZRERRFURRAF-
ERR
Shona regards the slacks with distaste
and repeats . . .
APERRAREMRERR?
Clearly she considers the slacks to be
unfashionable and tells her mother . . .
APERRAREMRERRZMERRFURRAS-
QUERR
The mother is determined to put on the
slacks and retires to a changing-room.
When she reappears in the tight-fitting
garment she is scrutinised by her
daughter who gasps . . .
BIGUMMUMSUMTUMANBUMMUM
Then Shona resumes her struggle to get
into the ra-ra skirt. Suddenly there is a
loud rending sound. From the mother

comes the anguished cry . . .
YURERSIZ!
With the addition of a word she reveals
the full extent of the catastrophe . . .
YURERSIZOOTRANARRARARA!

14 High-risibility

My friend Hughie who lives on the twentieth floor of a high-rise block in the new Gorbals is a keen observer of the Glasgow scene and likes to tell of events that go on around him.

Here he is in full flow . . .

You know, it's amazing the different types of people you find in a big block of flats . . .

There was Willie McStay, the bachelor chap on the tenth floor. Willie was a nice chap – but he had pedestrian eyes, they looked both ways before crossing. He was that skelly-eyed that no girl would look at him. He was so depressed about that that he decided to commit suicide. He went away down to Jamaica Bridge one summer's day, climbed up on the parapet and jumped. But him

being so squinty-eyed he jumped the wrong way. Landed flat on his back on the pavement. 'Just ma luck!' he said. 'The Clyde frozen over in June.' Then he realised his mistake. So he climbed up on the parapet again and he was just going to jump when a policeman arrived. The policeman knew Willie. 'Don't jump, Willie!' he yelled. 'If you jump into the water I'll have to jump in after you and I canny swim. If I try to rescue you I'll drown!' 'I'm gonny jump,' said Willie. 'Aw, have a heart,' said the bobby. 'If I drown, ma wife and seven weans'll have nobody to support them.' 'I'm gonny jump,' said Willie. 'No! Hang on a minute, Willie,' yelled the policeman, 'I've got an idea. The water doon there's cold and dirty. Why don't you go back to your nice wee bachelor flat and hang yourself in comfort?'

But Willie McStay didn't commit suicide. He found a girl who'd marry him, Big Annie. He met her while he was out jogging. He tripped over her guide dog. They had nine children and when the tenth baby arrived the neighbours clubbed together and gave them a lovely silver salver with their family crest on it. Big Annie was puzzled by the crest. 'What's that funny-looking duck on it?' 'That's not a duck,' said Wee Lizzie, 'That's a stork with its legs worn aff.'

Then there's Mrs O'Rourke on the first floor. I got a shock when I dropped in on her for a cup of tea. 'Heavens, Mrs O'Rourke,' I said. 'I didn't know you were an Orangewoman!' 'Sure and Oi'm no' an Orange-woman!' says she. Then I pointed at a statue on her mantelshelf. I asked her, 'What are you doing with a statue of King Billy on horseback?' She gaped at it. 'King Billy?!' she says, 'Wait till I get my hands on that wee Pakistani pedlar! He told me it was Lester Piggott!'

When the wee pedlar arrived here from Pakistan he got

a job on the buses. He was taught to drive, then the inspector sent him out on a brand-new, one-man, pay-as-you-enter bus. Twenty minutes later the inspector got an urgent 'phone call. The one-man double-decker bus had crashed. He dashed to the scene and he got a shock when he saw that the double-decker had crashed into the front of a pub. The wee Pakistani driver was leaning against the bus smoking a fag. 'How did *this* happen?' the inspector shouted at him. 'Goodness gracious, Mr Inspector, it is not my fault that the bus is crashing itself into the public house,' says the wee Pakistani driver. 'When it happened I was upstairs collecting the fares.'

There's never a dull moment in our high-rise block. The young married woman across the landing from Mrs O'Rourke had triplets the other day. Mrs O'Rourke went over to congratulate her. The young mother was awfully proud of her three bonnie babies. 'It's most unusual to have triplets,' she said. 'The doctor told me that it only happens once in two hundred thousand times.' 'Once in two hundred thousand times?!' said Mrs O'Rourke. 'When did ye find time to do yur hoosework?'

But, you know, there are some right bad wee rascals in the flats. I heard Gary and his pal Pete talking outside my door. Gary said, 'I had a rare night last Saturday. I wrecked a chip shop, assaulted the owner, sprayed paint all over the place and grabbed two fivers from the till. Then the polis nicked me.' Pete asked him, 'How did ye get on in the court, Gary?' 'Okay,' said Gary, 'ma murra spoke up for me. She said I was well brought up and had a luvly nature and would never do anything wrong.' 'Did ye get off?' asked his pal. 'Ayre sure,' says Gary, 'all that happened was ma murra got nine months for perjury.'

I was telling you about Willie the bachelor who took a long time to find a wife. Well, his brother Stevie had a very unhappy experience. Willie and his wife brought along this girl as a blind date for Stevie. But Stevie didny like the look of his blind date. The four of them were sitting in a pub and he whispered to Willie – 'This is a deid liberty! You told me this girl was young and she's forty if she's a day. You sayed she was beautiful and she's got a face on her like an ape. You sayed she was slim and she's as fat as a whale.' 'Whit the hell are ye whisperin' fur?' said Willie, 'she's stone deif an' a'.'

I'm sorry to say that a lot of the fellas in our block are unemployed. Two of them were walking along the street when they found a pay-poke. It was full, hadn't been opened. They decided to hand it in at the police office. But on the way there they came to a pub. 'Let's just have one wee hauf out of the pay-poke,' said one of the chaps. And into the pub they went. Well, one wee hauf led to another . . . and another . . . and another. It was very near closing time when they were flung out. They looked at the empty pay-poke and one of them complained, 'If the bugger who lost this had worked overtime we'd have enough for a cairry-oot.'

Aw but the great character in our block is wee Mrs McChleary. She's mad on bingo. She even has a motto hanging above her bed – 'Bless This Housey-Housey' . . . She's a widow. Her husband worked in a distillery. One day he slipped and fell into a vat of whisky. Died with a smile on his face. She told me that her husband had always been very tender . . . No wonder he was tender. She had him in hot water for forty years.

Now wee Mrs McChleary lives alone with her parrot. Oh, it's a cheeky bird, that parrot! I remember the time her sink got choked up and she sent for the plumber to come and clear it. She waited in for him for two days and he didn't appear. Then, when she was out at the bingo, the plumber turned up. He knocked at the door and the parrot screeched, *'who izzit?'*

The man said, 'It's the plumber. I've come to clear the choked sink. But again the parrot screeched, *'who izzit?'*

'It's the plumber,' the man called, 'I've come to clear the choked sink.' But all the parrot would say was *'who izzit?'*

The plumber was desperate. 'Don't you understand?' he shouted. 'It's me, the plumber. I've come to clear the choked sink.' The parrot screeched back, *'who izzit?'*

After the parrot had shrieked *'who izzit?'* twenty times the plumber got absolutely fed up. He sat down outside the door and soon he was sound asleep. And when Mrs McChleary got back from the bingo she didn't notice him sprawled there and she tripped over him. *'Who izzit?'* she yelled. And from inside the house the parrot screeched, 'It's the plumber. He's come to clear the choked sink.'

15 *Matturopattur*

A Scottish BBC official announced that sub-titles might be used in a documentary being made about the East End of Glasgow.

At once I was ready to offer the following modest glossary of picturesque expressions used by many of the natives of Glasgow.

HOWZITGAUN? HULLAWRERR! or AWSHURSEL?

How do you do?

AMNOTOOBAD or AVFELTWURSUR.

I am feeling quite well.

GOARAFAGOANYEMAC?

Can you spare me a cigarette?

AVHEEHAWFAGSLEF.

I have no cigarettes.

GOARAMDRI! AVVADROUTHOANME, or
ACUDGOAPINT.

I am very thirsty.

ERRAFELLASTOCIOUS, RATGUYSBEVVIED or
EEZMIROCLOUS.

That gentleman has wined rather well.

ERRAPERRAHERRIES.

There are two flamboyant young ladies.

AMGETTINRACUMOAN.

One young lady is looking coyly at me.

ALGIERA BURDRABURD.

I shall ignore her amorous advances.

CUMOANDOONTIRABARRAS.

Let us purchase some inexpensive gift.

WHIRRABOORATIGHTNUR?

I suggest that we have a meal.

MEFURRACOUPLAPIES.

I should like to eat some typically Scottish
fare.

SUMKYTE YIVGOATOANYE!

Alas I fear I am rather overweight!

STUFFYURTURKI!

Bon appetit!

SAPERRACOONCILLURS.

Those two gentlemen are wealthy intellectuals.

AWGOASHAMSKINT.

I regret to inform you that I am financially
embarrassed.

GONNILENZAPOUN?

Can you temporarily improve my cash flow?

WHISSAGEMME?

What makes you adopt that course of action?

SARERRTERRATRAFERR.

Glasgow Fair must be an enjoyable time.

AMDAMPTWABBITANCRABBIT!
> I am most annoyed when I feel tired!

REMCOARNSAMINES GIENMIGYP.
> My feet are quite painful.

YURPATTURZGOATMAHEIDGONROON!
> At times your language is quite
> incomprehensible!

*   *   *

With the arrival here of many English and foreign holidaymakers the big topic of conversation in Scotland will be the weather.

Some language difficulties may arise for those strangers in our midst.

Will they understand the natives when they are describing the vagaries of our climate?

In a bid to help the tourists over their linguistic problems, here are some of the obscure expressions used in connection with the weather in Scotland.

Of course there are the customary meteorological greetings like 'Snoabad dayraday', 'Sarerrmoarnin', 'Soffiwaarm', 'Whirra weekenda rain!', 'Rottenday-intit?' and 'Riswerra widscunnerye'.

But there are other and even more quaint words and phrases. Such as SANGAVA, used in the traditional phrase —

SANGAVA KOLRADAY.
> I am glad I did not dispense with my winter
> semmit.

Then we have:

RASUNZOOT!
> A miracle has happened!

SUNSANGAVAHOAT.
> The solar rays have raised my temperature.

TWIDGIEYERABOAK.
> This inclement weather is most depressing.

WHERRZANEARESTPUB?
> Where shall we shelter?

RAINZWENTAFF.
> The rain has stopped.

*   *   *

Glasgow people, on their return from holiday, use a special language when proudly showing the artistic examples of their photographic expertise.

For the benefit of those not acquainted with this technical parlance, let me give a few of these phrases and their meanings.

WANNYSEE WURPHOTIES?
> Are you prepared for an hour of utter boredom?

RATSMURRA PAIDLIN.
> Mother, in an undignified posture, bathing her feet.

SHOULDNYA TOOKRAT.
> Mother protesting at having been photographed.

WEEFELLA BELLAFELLINWI.
> A diminutive gentleman who made the acquaintance of Bella.

ERRAT OLSCUNNUR.
> Portrait of our landlady.

WIDGIE LOOKAT ROLYIN.
> Observe grandfather's open mouth as he sleeps in a deck-chair.

ATTAKA NOFFIPHOTY.

    Photographs never flatter me.

AMAZFATTAZAT?

    I don't believe the saying, 'The camera never
    lies.'

RATWIZTOOK UNAWERRS.

    I was not aware that this rearward view of me
    bending was being taken.

VIEWFAE WURROOM.

    Still-life study of brick wall with dustbins.

BIGBABSBAKIN OANRABEACH.

    Not a stranded whale, but Barbara
    sunbathing.

BOABMABRURRA INRARUBBLE.

    My brother Robert trying to enter his hotel at
    Benidorm.

RAWEAN FLINGIN SAUN.

    The child merrily throwing sand about.

MAFEYRA SKELPIN RAWEAN.

    My father cutting short the child's enjoyment.

WHOZARRAGAIN?

    I have forgotten the identity of that young
    lady.

SABURD SAMMYFELLOOTWI.

    It is the avaricious maiden on whom Samuel
    spent much of his holiday cash.

RATSASNAPIA RATIACHAP.

    That is a photograph of a holiday escort with
    whom I became disillusioned.

RATCHAP WAANTITATAP.

    He tried to negotiate with me for a loan.

BIGBABS INFURRADOOK.

    The tidal wave effect is caused by Barbara
    bathing.

OTHERRAPICNIC.

Here is a group photograph of the picnic party.

MAMAW YELLINUR HEIDAFF.

My mother has inadvertently sat upon a wasp.

POLLIZ PEELLIWALLIWILLI.

Polly's husband, William, after coming off the Big Dipper at Blackpool.

NAWTHEMSNOA PERRAHAMS.

No, it is not a study of two Belfast hams but a picture of Big Sandra in a mini-skirt.

Of course there are times when a holiday snapshot doesn't quite come up to standard.

On those occasions we are apt to hear the phrases:

MANTYKATE SATOANMA KODAK.

My Aunt Kate failed to notice the camera on the chair.

WURHEIDZIZCUTAFF.

Uncle Hughie had had a few refreshments before taking this photograph.

Hope the above will be of some help to those caught up in photographic developments. Orrabest — and WATCHRABURDICHINAS!

16 The Aspirants

Some young Glasgow men and women have ambitions to enter the world of entertainment. Quite a few come from the less salubrious parts of the city and their spartan upbringing toughens them and spurs them on to achieve great things.

Generally their careers are pursued outwith the city. Here are accounts of the struggles of two young people of my acquaintance:

Bunny girl? Whit a career! These auld playboys make ye career all over the place. Wan look at ma cotton wool tail and their hormones are workin' overtime. It seems they're never too auld. Last night one of them told me he was a sexagenarian. By Goad he wizny far wrong! He hirpled after me shouting 'I'm going to trap you, fair rabbit!' Then he collapsed, fair wabbit . . .

Of course it's no' easy gettin' to be a Bunny. I had to get an audition. A buncha Americans. The auldest yin was the expert on figures. Eyes like a perra glass bools. You shoulda seen him runnin' them up and doon ma development area. I was embarrassed. I told him – 'Take yer eyes aff ma legs!' 'Oh,' he says, 'I'm above that.' Then he sayed he wanted to see ma credentials. 'Naw,' says I, 'Ye're seein' a' ye're gonny see!' . . .

Oh I was awful nervous! I asked him if I had the right to apply for the job. 'Sure!' he says, 'ye've a perfect right.' 'I know,' says I, 'but whit's wrang wi' ma left?'

Next he asked me if I had the mentality of a Bunny. So I told him ma family was hare-brained . . . bred like rabbits. Oh aye, there was twenty-two of us. Ma mother went up tae the Housing Department to see aboot a new hoose. The man told her – 'It's no' a hoose you want, it's a hutch.'

Anyway I got the job in the Jollyboy Club. Funny place that. The customers are no' allowed tae lay a finger on ye. Oh what a difference from the job I had in Glasgow. I was a waitress in a business men's coffee room . . . Naw, in the Jollyboy Club they're only allowed tae look at ye, chat ye up an' they're that frustrated they get fu'. It's a case o' keek, cheek an' then they get seeck.

Oh but some of them are as bold as brass. There was wan auld lech. Seventy-five years auld and rich. Oh he had mair money than a Cabinet Minister. He carried on like a reckless young blood – and he looked like a bloodless auld wreck. He took an awfy notion to one of our Bunny girls, Marlene McGubbin. Ye'll no' credit it. She married that auld josser of seventy-five! And she was only nineteen. I told her – 'It's like an auld pop star marryin' a young thing. Ye're shairly no' expectin' him tae sing?' 'Naw,' she sayed, 'I'm expectin' him tae croak.'

Oh ye meet them in the Jollyboy Club. One wee American tourist came in. He spent fifty pounds on me! So I took him home for a . . . cuppa cocoa. Well, he came back the next night and spent another fifty pounds on me. So I took him home again. Well ye'll no' believe it. He came in a third night and spent another fifty pounds. I sayed to him, 'Here, you've been in three nights runnin' and ye've spent fifty pounds on me each time. Ye must be loadit!' 'Oh no,' he sayed, 'I'm just a poor li'l plumber from New York City.' 'New York City?' sayed I, 'I've a brother that stays there!' 'I know,' he sayed, 'He gave me one hundred and fifty pounds to give to you.'

Right anough, some of these Yanks would gi'e ye the boak. The worst yins are the ones that used tae belong tae Glasgow. A year in the States an' they come back wearin' big Stetson hats an' talkin' like J. R. Ewing.

Big Basil was like that. He strolls inty the club, looks doon at me, then he says, 'Say, babe, Ah'm half-inclined to kiss you!' 'Is that whit it is?' says I, 'I thought ye were humphy-backit.'

Ach it's no' a bad life in the Jollyboy Club. Mind ye, some of the bunnies are cats. Take big Samantha McGurk. Conceited as they make them. She went inty a beauty parlour and asked them to give her the Barbra Streisand Look. The hairdresser lifted his brush and bashed her wan on the face.

But the heid Bunny Girl's nice. We cry her the Mother Bunny. Poor sowl, she's awful troubled wi' her weight. She's on a new diet. She can eat anything she likes – but she's no' supposed tae swallow. It's a shame. Her figure's 62–24–19. Mind ye, wi' a bit o' help she can stand up.

I'm sorry for the Mother Bunny. A lot of sadness in her life. Oh aye. Her man, bends the elba, ye know . . . Oh he went an awfu' length! He'd do anything for a drink – except work for it. She had to sit at home at nights. Nae television. And she had nothing to read but pawn tickets.

Well there was nothing for it . . . divorce. She told the judge that durin' her marriage her man spoke to her only three times. Of course, she got the custody of the three weans.

She married again. Her saicint man gave her a lovely honeymoon. She told me they went all over Europe and America. First-class travel and first-class hotels. I sayed tae her – 'Your man must be a millionaire!' 'Naw,' she sayed, 'He's a Glasgow Town Councillor.'

Aw but the Mother Bunny's got a hard job. Ye see, she's got to keep us innocent. She was fair blazin' at a man in oor cabaret. He announced he was gonny sing a song about a little yellow bird. Then he gave us fourteen verses of 'Auntie Mary Had a Canary'. Whit a bloomer! We were black affronted.

It's a funny thing though – when ye've been a Bunny Girl for a while ye get sick of admiration. Ye want tae get married an' settle doon. Wee Lily Skelly was like that. A nice wee lassie – but she hudny the phyzzicue tae be a Bunny Girl. She found her tray o' fags an' whitnutt too heavy for her. It had a bad effect on her legs. She was the only bandy-leggit Bunny in the club.

Big Deirdre's a nice big sowl. Married six months and she's still crazy aboot her man. She was tellin' me about her honeymoon. 'Oh it was marvellous!' she says. 'We only stayed up late wance – tae watch *Coronation Street*.'

A week in Spain resulted in Sammy's aspiring to be a flamenco dancer. Here he tells how he began:

Listen, folks, I've a confession to make. I'm really not Spanish. I'm not from Madrid; I'm from Maryhill. Mind you, my mother says I've got Spanish blood in me. She called my father 'Don Juin' . . . He was never due in till dawn.

Actually I got into this Spanish dancing business by accident. Ye see, I'm in the linoleum trade. I am what is known as a linoleum-tramper-dooner. Ye know when ye put down a roll of linoleum. Take your eyes off it for a second and it comes curlin' back at ye as fast as a Glasgow bus going to the garage. Well, when the linoleum curls up like that I'm called in to tramp it down.

First of all I study the extent of the curling, then I place my spuds in position and commence to tramp with great velocity. As you see, this is a highly-skilled job.

Of course, that is only the elementary tecknicue. Sometimes a more advanced technicology is called for, especially when large bulges appear in the new-laid linoleum. When that happens I have to employ what we term THE BULGE SMOOTHER-OOTER.

Quite often linoleum curls up from *all* the walls of a room. So I have to use a very advanced tecknicue. It was invented by my friend, big Rudy Nooryeff. It's known as the BASH IT DOON WI' YUR BUNIONS step.

The *worst* emergency us tramper-dooners have to contend with is when the linoleum rises in waves. Great weight is needed to smooth out these waves. So, to get this weight, I have to partake of two plates of porridge, four pies and a large daud of sultana cake. Then I place myself on the linoleum and go into a special routine. It's called THE WAVE-REDUCING BURRLE.

Oh, but I'm forgetting the Spanish dancing. It all began when I went to the Linoleum-Tramper-Dooner's Conference in Madrid. I went with another linoleum-tramper, Stevie McSwain. But he went home after two days. He didn't like Spain. 'Ach the place is hoatchin' wi' Spaniards,' he said. 'An' they're helluva bad speakers. Ah canny make oot a bliddy word the buggers are sayin'.' But I stayed on in Madrid and there, in the Palace of Waxcloth, I gave an exhibition of linoleum-tramping. Mind you, it wasn't easy. Ye see, it gets that dampt hot in Spain that the linoleum comes up in waves.

Never have I saw such waves! I had to swallow half a bottle of Quells before I could walk on them. But I gritted my feet and conquered those waves. Then I was presented with a medal – the DSO . . . Distinguished Smoother-Ooter.

Then out of the blue came a cable from the Town Clerk of Glasgow. 'Fly home at once,' it said. 'We are re-laying the floors of the City Chambers.' They wanted me to tramp down the new linoleum!

What an honour! The last time they put down linoleum in the City Chambers the Lord Provost laid the first roll. All of a sudden it sprung back, wrapped itself round his corporation and went tearing down the marble staircase with the Lord Provost inside it. Then it took off and landed in a field near Edinburgh. Fortunately the Lord Provost made a soft landing . . . there'd been a cattle show in the field the day before.

Well, when I got that cable to return to Glasgow I dashed out to Madrid Airport. I was that excited! My feet were itching to get started on that new linoleum in the City Chambers! I was stamping away like mad. Then up comes a Spaniard. 'Caramba!' he says. 'No, the name's Simpson,' says I. 'Caramba!' he says again. 'You are a born Spanish dancer!' I tried to explain I was a linoleum-tramper-dooner. 'Maravilloso!' he cried, 'you have a flair for it!' 'Of course,' says I. 'Where d'ye think we put the linoleum?'

It turned out he was an impresario. 'Muy bueno Inglese!' he yells . . . he was an awful sweerer . . . 'I will make you a star!' I asked him, 'How can you make me a star, seenyur?' 'Seenyur no' everybody,' he says. And before ye could say 'manana' he rushed me along to his nightclub and introduced me to a big dark dame. 'This is your dancing partner,' he says, 'La Cascara Sagrada.'

Well, La Cascara fairly kept me on the go. What a dancer. She didn't need castanets. Every time she stamped her feet her wallies clicked. It was like listening to the turnstiles at Hampden.

What an exhibition of dancing we gave! Tarantella, sevillana, rumba, paso doble, passa Lanliq . . . It was all the same to us. I was fair biling . . . Then came disaster. The big Spanish impresario shouted 'Ole! Ole!' and wheeched me up in the air. Ma heel caught in his cummerbund and I landed flat on my fandango.

And that's how my career began.

17 *Put-down an'nat*

When I was a lad a brusque remark intended to silence the listener was known as a 'squelch'. In modern parlance it is a 'put-down' or 'knock-back'.

Many Glaswegians are adept at administering the put-down.

The late and great Scottish actor, Duncan Macrae was wont to indulge in this art.

He was in a play in London with Laurence Olivier and Orson Welles, who also directed the production. I asked Macrae how he'd got on with the two great actors.

'Aw, Larry's a *gentleman*,' he said, 'But see that Orson Welles . . . a big chancer'.

Molly Urquhart, the accomplished actress who left 'straight' acting to become a highly-successful comedienne was at the receiving end of a particularly disconcerting put-down. Her first appearance in a lavish 'Half-Past Eight' revue at the Theatre Royal, Glasgow, was a great success. The audience warmed to her and she received a standing ovation.

Applause and cheers still ringing in her ears and laden with bouquets of flowers, she returned to the flat where she lived with her widowed father.

She rang the doorbell and the door was at once flung open. Before Molly could utter a word about her triumph the old gentleman barked at her, 'Do you know there's no' a slice o' breid in this hoose?'

The Glaswegian put-down often includes the word 'achawan' which can be translated into the English 'Oh, go away and . . .'

So a tiresome person might be put down with such rebukes as '*Achawan* take a runnin' jump tae yursel'' '*Achawan* bile yur can' or, if the person is excessively annoying, '*Achawan* bile yur heid'.

Other peculiarities may be noted in Glaswegian speech patterns.

There is the strange use of the word 'there' – pronounced *therr*. 'Ah wiz alang at the City Chambers therr,' someone will state. The word 'therr' has nothing to do with the location of the City Chambers. It is merely added as a kind of emphasis in the sentence. 'She landit oan hur bum when she wiz tryin' tae ski in the Cairngoarms therr'.

'But' and 'and that' – pronounced 'an' nat' also feature in some Glaswegian conversations.

The use of these words is illustrated in the following dialogue between our two 'windae-hingin'' friends, Maggie and Sarah:

MAGGIE: See that big wumman that steys oan the toap flat therr?

SERAH: Aye.

MAGGIE: Hur lassie's gettin' married.

SERAH: Gettin' married? She's terrible fat, but. See black puddins? She can eat three at wan go.

MAGGIE: It's a good thing she likes black puddins an'nat, her intendit works in the black puddin factory therr.

SERAH: Ye wonder whit he sees in hur.

MAGGIE: If he looked doon hur throat he'd see a hunner black puddins. She's the youngest of the big wumman's ten weans. Hur murra's ran oota names. She dizny know whit tae call hur husband next.

SERAH: Ah better away in. Ah've goat a big pie an'nat in the oven. Ma brother an' his wife are comin' fur thur tea. She's a bit poash, but. She dizny take hur rubbidge an'nat tae a midden, she sends them tae the Cleansin' Department by parcel post. Ah'll away an' see tae the pie therr. Cheery-bye ra noo.

18 *Tales of the Tipplers*

The Glaswegian in stage, radio and television plays is not infrequently portrayed as a raucous drunk. Not so. Only a small minority of the citizens behave in an unseemly fashion after imbibing.

Nevertheless the consumption of alcohol has a fascinating patois all of its own.

A gentleman who has indulged himself rather too liberally may be described as 'stocious', 'bevvied', 'stovin'', 'jaked', 'miroclous', 'smugged' or 'paralytic'.

These terms are rarely applied to ladies. When one of the more abstemious sex is, as the phrase has it, 'partial to a refreshment', she is described as 'merry' or 'having a wee glow on'.

A gentleman who has done himself rather well at the

bar but doesn't show the effects of his libations is described in complimentary terms as 'haudin' it well' or having a 'guid bead in him'.

Glasgow hostelries are cheerful places and the air rings with such pleasant inquiries as 'Whit ur ye fur?' 'Ur ye fur annurra?' 'D'ye waant a big yin?'

Glasgow women do not regard too censoriously their husbands' drinking proclivities. One especially tolerant lady was heard to declare, 'Hughie's fondia hauf'.

The word 'fondia' is employed in such statements as 'He's fondia guid bucket', 'She's fondia big vodka' and 'They're fondia laugh'.

I hope, dear reader, that you are in the latter category and that you've found a laugh or two in this book.

Acknowledgements

The photograph on p. 6 is reproduced by kind permission of Mr John Schlesinger, the photograph on p. 126 by kind permission of the BBC, and the photographs on pp. 12, 22, 26, 30, 32, 42, 52, 72 and 82 by kind permission of London Weekend Television. The remaining photographs are from Mr Baxter's private collection.